Understand… …eople

A Handboo… …ightworkers

Genn John

Understanding the Crystal People: A Handbook for Lightworkers

Cover creation and design by Kent Hesselbein

Back cover photo credit and crystal location by Fenix Deroche in Jessieville, Arkansas

Illustrations by Genn John

ISBN 978-1-935786-68-9

Printed in the United States of America by

St. Clair Publications

PO Box 726

McMinnville, TN 37111-0726

http://stclairpublications.com/

Reviews

Taking a walk through *Understanding The Crystal People: A Handbook for Lightworkers* was educational, enlightening and entertaining. There is so much to comprehend when one wishes to become a crystal guardian; even with my sizeable collection, I gleaned much knowledge from the reading of this book. Genn's writing style is one that is peppered with visual examples (which were incredibly helpful to me) and stories from her past (which we can all learn from), all mixed together with a keen sense of humor (which is food for the soul); there were times when I found myself chuckling right along with her. Having known Genn for a great many years, I trust her, implicitly, when it comes to locating the very crystal that I am looking for. It is my privilege to be able to heartily endorse this magnificent book.

Michele Doucette, author of *The Wisdom of Crystals* and *Healing the Planet and Ourselves: How To Raise Your Vibration*

Understanding The Crystal People is so much more than a book about crystals. A must read for all Lightworkers, and anyone who has ever felt drawn to the subtle energy of crystals, this book teaches us, through the profound and ancient wisdom of the Crystal People, how to reconnect with

ourselves (which also includes our own Divine purpose) and Gaia. Genn's reverence for the Crystal People, important work in bringing them to light, in direct association with the immense knowledge that she gains from working alongside them, is illuminated in this powerful read. Written in Genn's humorous and warm way of Being, a format that is easy to understand, *Understanding The Crystal People* also incorporates practical advice and tools on how we can implement the teachings.
Meg Adams, Social Media Specialist and Viral Publicist

Genn John is far more than an experienced resource for guidance about crystal. The knowledge she has acquired, from her lifelong bond with these amazing stones, is shared on every page, but what makes this book invaluable is her ability to help you understand the crystals you have brought into your life and why you selected them (or rather, why you responded when they chose to call out to you). Genn combines an unassuming manner, a rollicking sense of humor, and a literally out-of-this-world connection with crystal. We have all become aware of the horse and dog whisperers within our midst; through the very pages of *Understanding The Crystal People*, we now have access to Genn John, the renowned Crystal Whisperer!
Patricia Walton, Clairvoyant and Spiritual Medium

Table of Contents

Acknowledgments

I am thankful to my parents and soul family for blessing me with such an awesome support team. I can't think of anyone I would have rather had in my corner, cheering me on and bolstering my confidence.

I am eternally grateful to my dear friends who helped me through numerous edits, Angel Walton and Michele Doucette. Thank you for sharing your grammatical wisdom.

Angel, thank you for patiently reading through the manuscript countless times so that by the time Michele received it, it was readable. Michele, I consider myself privileged and blessed that you have shared so much of your hard-earned knowledge to help me see this book through to print. Thanks aren't enough for the assistance you have so graciously and tirelessly provided.

To my crystal friends, the wonderful people who have adopted their crystal babies from Arkansas Crystal Works, I am both honored and awed to have been trusted with such a sacred mission. I consider myself lucky beyond belief to have the privilege of calling so many of you "friend."

Most importantly, I am humbled and eternally indebted to these ancient beings, the Crystal People, for allowing me the honor of acting as their legs for so many years and for the new opportunity to be their voice as well. I look forward to walking and talking with them into the future.

Message from the Crystal People

I've been asked by Genn to add my thoughts to this book.

Firstly, we are thrilled that she finally decided to put our words down for others to read.

We've been speaking to her so long that it is nice to be able to share our thoughts with the people who have been in contact with her.

Genn has asked us for any comments and thoughts we may have regarding the concepts in this fine book, and also if we had a message for humanity, coming into these new energies.

Lastly, she wanted us to go over anything we'd like to add that she may have missed.

We are thrilled to be able to assist her in this way and thank you for the opportunity to share!

To begin we would like to express our gratitude that the desire is there for you to learn more about us and to do your best to understand our thoughts as it were.

You see we are similar to you in many ways, but different also.

Where shall we begin?

Our message for you is that while this is a time of great change, which can be a frightening thing, it is also a time for great excitement because the potential for growth is tremendous. Indeed, we have also been waiting a long time for this moment.

The accomplishment of our mission requires humanity to understand how we work and function in order for us to do the most good (if we are to assist humanity). Does this make sense?

While we are quite capable of assisting our great mother Gaia, in her ascension, in order to assist humanity you have to be able to tune into our wavelength.

While it is possible to connect with us from a distance, as the channel, Genn, and many others do, it is indeed an advanced practice and takes time to master.

This is why it is important for us to be physically present with you for the greatest good at this point.

This requires that we come out of our space in the warm earth and enter the light.

It is a somewhat painful process, not unlike your human birth. Genn talks about this later.

On a grander scale, however, it is time that we emerge; that we have the assistance of your human legs to deliver us globally.

As shared earlier, we are always working from where we are, but it is of assistance to most that we are near.

Genn has also asked us to talk about something which we have been discussing, which she asked us to explain here.

The subject is where we come from, not our physical bodies, but our light bodies.

We've been discussing with her that our existence is very similar to your human existence; at least where what you term the Soul or Spirit is concerned.

The mineral crystal (the body) is something we inhabit, because its vibration is so high, and its ability to accept our vibration so perfect. We could no more function (in the physical realm) without our physical bodies than humanity.

Of course, we also function on astral levels and different non physical planes without our physical form, just as you do.

Our physical lifespan is so much longer than yours, as a human, simply because the physical vehicle we have chosen is longer lasting.

The physical structure, while much more dense than your vehicle of flesh and blood, is of an infinitely higher vibration; so in fact, we are lighter.

Like you, we experience different levels of "age", some of us younger and some older.

Given that our physical life span is so much longer than the human life span, it can become difficult for us to explain and for you to understand.

In imagining how long we are in our physical crystalline body, perhaps you are able to better understand it when we share that this is but one of our many lifetimes.

This is why you see us as so much more wise than you; indeed, we are ancient beyond your knowing or comprehension.

Genn wanted us to explain where we come from, and from where we originate, but we can no more do that than we can tell you from where you originate; not because we don't know, but because it is beyond the ability of our dear Genn, as a channel, to comprehend.

We don't have a point of reference to give her for a proper translation.

We are of the stars, as are you.

We are simply thrilled that we have been able to share this knowledge with you and we look forward to spending time with you in the future.

We wanted to discuss a little bit about why we are here, in these mountains you call the Ouachitas, and in the state you call Arkansas.

Long, long ago during the time of Atlantis, and even further back to Lemuria (Mu), the place we called the Motherland, humanity had what you now call Lightworkers; many were Healers, and others, the Priests.

They had very advanced knowledge of us and knew how to grow our crystalline form.

Under these mountains in Arkansas the conditions were perfect for the placement of a nursery of sorts; a garden, if you will.

They planned this area, seeded it for their use then, but more for the future they knew was coming.

That future is your present.

Many of you reading this will remember your lifetimes during those civilizations, some of you will have latent memories which will awaken, or come to the working surface of your minds, when your vibration raises and it is the time during your soul contract in which you are to remember.

Some of you experience these memories as dreams and tell yourself it is imagination or fantasy; we are here to assure you, it is not.

There are also great crystalline forms, Earthkeepers, which were placed for safekeeping.

For the protection of humanity, and indeed the world, it was required that these great crystalline forms be hidden and made inaccessible until the proper time. They are to be found deep beneath the surface in places such as your Mount Magazine, that which you call Eureka Springs, beneath the ridge at what you call Talimena as well as other places around the globe, but for the purpose, and intent, of this book, we speak only of the Arkansas crystal matrix.

Indeed, we are a matrix. We are all connected (the crystalline energies such as myself) which is why we appear (speak here) in plural and not singularly.

While this message is indeed coming through that which my dear friends have named Venus, while she is a separate individual, she is also, and at the same time, One with us all.

Simply, we select a singular to speak because it would be difficult for you to understand our message otherwise.

Being connected in this way, we are able to communicate with our brothers and sisters globally (and indeed, beyond), beneath your mountains, to what you call Brazil and Tibet and all over.

We connect with one another as fast as a thought; quicker than that, even. Much like your internet or cell phones, but much, much faster and far more efficiently.

So in truth, Dear Ones, we don't need to come out of the Earth in order for our mission to be carried out. We can do what we need to do from where we are.

As a matter of fact, while we ARE in the Earth, while our crystalline bodies are in the Earth, manipulating vibrations and energy, we reside primarily OUT of the Earth; in another plane where we are able to work equally from both places.

Since the time is now that we are needed to help raise the vibration of humanity, we have chosen to enter our crystalline form bodies, en masse, to act as a conduit between our thought energy and what you can comprehend.

Much like your television and radio waves, you are not physically able to decipher the signals unless you have the proper box to pick up the frequency; so, too, must you be able to translate this frequency into something which you can understand.

This is the role our crystalline bodies play for us.

We aren't "born" from that seed, with our consciousness trapped in the vessel until we are born to the light.

We are present and we are not.

While the great beds grow, and develop, we visit, tend, nurture, and increase vibrations, constantly moving; we work as a whole from this less dense plane.

When it is time for our birth, bits of us divide off to reside in these separate earth bodies, while still remaining quite connected to the One. It is why the different shapes that you call Record Keepers or Isis Face, or many of the other varied names and varieties identified, can each, and every one, do what the other can.

We are all one. Do you follow?

While a Record Keeper, or another shaped configuration, may be considered to serve a specific role which the current Lightworkers (and by current, Dear Ones, we mean perhaps hundreds even thousands of your human years) have agreed that they resonate better with, energies are expected to be found within these specific crystalline forms mainly because the structure is such that certain vibrations transmit more freely within, so we choose to enhance, and work through, those energies and manifest in that way.

However, each crystalline being retains what they know from their countless lifetimes, as well as having access to the One, always.

While we are partly of the One, we are also as you are in individual form with different personalities.

Some of us are what you would describe as more playful, some more what you would call serious, or even gruff, but Dear Ones, this is just a perception and there is always, always and without exception, great love, warmth and concern for your wellbeing.

Beyond all other things, we love you and wish to be of service in the best way possible.

There will come a day when you can connect to us, the One, or as individuals without the need for our crystalline form; this is why we have prompted Genn, our dear friend and advocate, to finally put this knowledge in written form.

It is our wish that more of you will awaken to the great possibility, the great probability, that you will learn to hear our language, feel our thought vibration, from a distance, both individually as well as collectively, and to tap into our great grid, sending our energies to where they are best needed for both personal and global healing.

We thank Genn, our dear channel, our friend, both for her courage and for allowing us this wonderful opportunity.

We thank her human guides, and helpers, for supporting her, for in helping her, they are helping us.

So many wonderful humans have connected with us over the span of humanity's lifetimes and for that we are eternally grateful and thankful.

Our love for you is immense and boundless.

We walk hand in hand with you, in joy, into this new era of ascending vibrations on your Earth walk.

We are here to be of service: service to each other, service to humanity, service to our great mother Gaia, service to the furry, feathered, finned, and skinned, the few legged and the many legged, the plant people; service to all.

We welcome your assistance in this great transition, this raising of vibration, this increase of love light.

We both thank you and bid you fond farewell until we connect again, which is all an illusion, anyway.

We reside with you permanently in this sacred NOW moment, which is both past and present, all times and places at once.

We leave you in this eternal NOW moment with shimmery blessings and embraces of light from us.

– VENUS, Crystal Guide, speaking on behalf of the Crystal People

About the Book

Crystal People … what a concept!

I know if you're reading this book you consider yourself a crystal person. The Crystal People I am speaking of, however, are the crystals themselves; sentient beings millennia older than ourselves!

A new energy is arriving. We're moving out of an era of following others' authority and more fully into following self-directed, intuitive guidance.

In this book you will learn how to listen to the crystal in your own way, rather than hearing their voice through someone else's filter. I will teach you what you need to know in order to do this.

You will learn where the crystal comes from, how they are formed and what language they speak.

You will learn how to speak that language and how to connect with your crystal friend.

I know that many of you have read the names of the different quartz configurations, but I suspect that some of you may still be finding it difficult to determine, with absolute certainty, what YOUR crystal is and how to best put it to use for personal and global healing.

Many books list so many different possible uses for each configuration that it is difficult (if not impossible) to remember the strongest ability of each type of crystal.

I have listed several common configurations, providing you with both detailed descriptions, as well as drawings, to further help you identify your crystal friends.

I will teach you a step-by-step method for reading the physical characteristics of your crystal.

In having included one or two uses for each configuration, I have also left room for you to record your own impressions and experiences.

It is much more important that you determine how each crystal type works for you rather than depending on the opinions of others.

You will learn how to cleanse, clear and program your crystal.

I have suggested many different uses that include healing, gridding and energy amplification, among others.

I have also taken the time to cover where you may find crystals and even how to gather your own.

Are you ready to embark on your journey?

Let's go!

My Introduction to the Crystal People

Grandparents who are rock hounds, well, rock!

I grew up in California and spent my formative years scrambling up hills, running wild in the mountains and combing the beaches.

We looked for square nails and purple bottles at old home sites, hematite and gold in the mountains, and agate on the beaches of the Pacific Northwest.

My grandparents were collectors and if I was lucky I got to tag along.

They used to gather Arkansas crystal and ship it back home to California. I remember growing up looking at crystal clusters sparkling and shining in the California sunshine.

Little did I know that I would become friends with these majestic beings!

How lucky am I? How lucky are you? I'm going to teach you to connect, but, alas, I am getting ahead of myself.

Let me start from the very beginning of my journey.

Besides rocks and collecting, art has been my passion my entire life. I began my path as an adult majoring in the fields of Fine Art and Graphic Design.

After hearing so many people ask me what in the world I was going to do with a Degree in Art, and internalizing all of the negative reasons why this was a bad choice, I abandoned my dream and entered the field of Nursing.

My mother was a nurse, several aunts were nurses. It was the logical step, or so I thought, but logic and happiness don't always go hand in hand.

Nursing isn't my path. While being a healer and nurturer IS, Nursing is not.

Don't get me wrong, I was a great nurse. I graduated at the top of my class and made a perfect score on my State Board Exam. Still, I was a very unhappy person following this path, which, clearly, was not for me.

Soldiering on, however, I worked as a Licensed Practical Nurse while continuing my education towards my Bachelor's Degree in Nursing.

I was nearly finished with college when I discovered that, physically, something was very wrong with me. I was sick with a laundry list of flu-like symptoms, chest and back pain, low grade fever and severe fatigue.

I made numerous trips to the student infirmary, took countless rounds of antibiotics and still there were no answers in sight to account for the symptoms I continued to have. Several months passed and I discovered a lump in my neck.

After more testing, which also included a biopsy, I was diagnosed with Hodgkin's Lymphoma –cancer.

The doctor who gave me the diagnosis said, “The bad news is you have cancer. The good news is this is the kind of cancer you'd want to have if you had to pick.”

I thought, “Really? I'd rather not have cancer at all; thanks just the same!”

However, cancer it was, and it was time to decide on treatment plans and what to do next. Being on the wrong path wasn't the issue any more; survival was.

I quickly found out that there's nothing quite like a cancer diagnosis to kick you out of the groove you've worn yourself into and back onto the right track.

Chemotherapy and radiation were the prescribed course of action. At that time, I didn't know anything about alternative medicine or treatments.

Being twenty-seven years old, the doctors decided to treat me very aggressively. In fact, they nearly killed me a few times.

Looking back, I can see how the Universe (or my Higher Self) was steering me back onto the right track, and to my soul contract, through this cancer diagnosis.

As I progressed through my treatment, alternative experiences were being brought to me gradually, and, *so I thought*, randomly.

While I was in the hospital, one of my nurses offered me a Reiki treatment for nausea, and to my surprise, it worked!

She started talking to me about a carved horse in one of the antique shops in town. She shared that she could feel the energy in the wood.

She must have seen something in me at that time that I didn't even know existed. Why else would a nurse, *seemingly out of the blue*, tell her patient about feeling vibrations in a piece of wood?

This was twenty years ago. I wasn't as in-tune with energy, or the idea of esoteric experiences as I am now. To be honest, as she talked, I nodded and smiled, but secretly I thought she was nuts!

A few months later, my home health nurse introduced me to Runes, Tarot and crystal grids.

I have always considered myself an open-minded person. It embarrasses me how, in hindsight, I had judged the first nurse who introduced the subject of subtle energy.

With my second nurse (thank you, Universe, for sending these two Angels), I was beginning to see these concepts in a new light.

Cancer drugs are in effect, poison. My body was unable to recover from the repeated assaults, which brought about a premature end to my treatments.

I felt such a wave of relief. I was so happy to be free of the chemotherapy! My hair was growing back and my energy was beginning to slowly increase.

Then, suddenly, the pain struck.

When I was really little, I remember playing in the snow on a family vacation. Following my older sister, I attempted to climb a small snow bank. While she scrambled up easily, I wasn't able to climb higher yet was afraid to let go.

I was hanging there like a monkey until I couldn't feel my hands. I was screaming and blubbering, numb hands stubbornly clinging to the snow bank. Rescuing me, my dad put me in the car with the heater on full blast and held my hands in the hot air from the vent, rubbing them together briskly.

Have you ever experienced this cold to hot transition? In case you haven't, I'll tell you how it feels … it's comparable to slamming your hands in the car door. All those nerve endings *scream* as they wake up.

Bringing us back to the chemotherapy, as my nerves rebounded from the assault, it wasn't just my hands as in the snow example; it was my entire body!

I don't have to tell you, the experience was Hell.

The treatment killed the cancer but it wasn't before causing irreparable nerve damage. As a result, I transitioned from the poison of chemotherapy to painkillers and anticonvulsant drugs in hopes of managing the constant pain.

The relief of being in remission turned to shock and then alarm at the realization of what had happened to my body during treatment.

Depression covered me like a wet wool blanket; heavy and inescapable. None of the many drugs I was prescribed helped.

I moved from the hill country of Kerrville, Texas to nearby Buchannan Dam.

I met some of the locals while house hunting. I told them I had just undergone treatment for cancer and was suffering from the after-effects. They mentioned the quartz in Lake Buchannan, near Marble Falls.

I told them I was familiar with the *beauty* of quartz crystal, but I didn't understand what that had to do with cancer.

They proceeded to tell me about the healing properties of quartz.

Initially, I was skeptical. However, I was more receptive to the notion than I was when introduced to the vibration in wood concept, and, quite frankly, I was willing to try anything.

I would have gladly strapped crystals to my head and clucked like a chicken if I thought it might help.

Thinking back to my childhood, I remembered my grandpa laughing as he told stories about the "hippies" who would sit with a box of crystal in their laps and "feel" each crystal until they found "just the right one." His description wasn't very complimentary. This is where I got the notion that people who did that were probably a little weird.

It is funny to look back at the old, un-awakened, Genn. I am so grateful that I woke up!

I was glad to learn about the properties of quartz crystal from my new friends. They told me the lake was full of quartz and kept reiterating how very healing it is.

No doubt about it, Lake Buchannan and the area surrounding is gorgeous, but it also has a deep, calm serenity.

I am certain this is because of the energy from the quartz.

Wading in the water of Lake Buchannan, and meditating on the porch overlooking the lake, I realized that my pain was slowly subsiding. Intellectually I didn't know how the crystals would figure in, but my higher Self knew I was finally coming home to my true path.

I started to paint and draw again.

The medications weren't doing anything except making me fuzzy-minded, so instead of taking the pills, I waded. I sat. I painted. I picked up the snowy quartz drusy anywhere I saw it.

Like the waves gently lapping on the shore, a quiet happiness washed over me. The wet blanket weight of depression began to lighten. The pain was decreasing and the joy I thought I'd lost, forever, slowly began to return.

My grandfather, living in Clarksville Arkansas, was ailing. My mom and I needed to move there to lend him a hand. Grandpappy was still rigid and cantankerous, but family is family, and when they need help, that's what you do, right?

Reluctantly, I left my healing, crystal-filled lake to embark on yet another leg of my journey.

Mom and I had decided that in every new place we lived we would do the things that the locals tended to take for granted, so we picked up shells on the Louisiana Gulf Coast, visited Sea World and the Alamo in Texas, and dug crystal in Arkansas.

We bought a tent and set out on a new adventure.

We started digging at the free Forest Service mine in Mount Ida, Arkansas. A mile hike up a steep trail led us to a mine that hadn't been worked for a very long time. We came away with just a few small points. Not being hikers, it was exhausting and disheartening, to say the least.

Luckily, we didn't stop after that first digging experience.

Spurring me on were the memories of the stories my Granny told me of their crystal digging trips. In the early „70's there were less restrictions and diggers were allowed into the working part of the mine. She spoke of crystal veins so large a person could walk into them, conjuring images of a dragon's lair lined in glowing crystal.

We tent-camped and dug at several different mines, and I came to discover that camping and crystal digging were my new favorite things! I wasn't overly thrilled with the tent part, though. Roughing it has its definite downsides, among them unpleasant campground bathrooms and having to build a fire from scratch when you're cold.

Tent-camping was often too hot, too cold or too wet, and it was always lots of work. While the camping part was difficult, we happily dug, dug, dug crystal to our heart's content.

Eventually, we discovered the answer to the inconvenience of tent camping; that answer was a recreational vehicle.

Mom and I, along with my long-haired Chihuahua, Ody, took full advantage of the luxuries it afforded. Avoiding the traditional discomforts, we had instant heat in the winter and air conditioning in the summer, all while enjoying the positive aspects of camping such as roasting marshmallows and being in the great outdoors.

Crystal digging was about all I wanted to do!

Let me tell you about Ody.

A rescue dog, Ody was estimated to be somewhere over ten years old. Four pounds soaking wet, he had no teeth which gave him the puckered grin of the toothless. His hair was wild, fluffy, yellow-white, and it stuck out in all directions. He had big shiny black eyes, one of which bore the blue-grey scar from a tangle with a cat.

He was the most wonderful companion and he LOVED to dig for crystals! Of course, he loved to be carried even more, so his “digging” was from the comfort of the inside of one of our shirts or on a “pillow” fashioned out of a shirt laid in the bucket on top of the crystal. He would grunt and complain every time we bent over.

My mom was an invaluable help when it came to cleaning and sorting. She deserves a great deal of credit along with my undying thanks for taking care of me when I was sick and enjoying time with me when I was well. Thanks, Mom!

Over the span of about two years, my health began to slowly decline. We never stopped digging because it always made me feel better, regardless. It was an obsession. My energy was higher at the crystal mines and my mood was always lighter.

During one of my routine check-ups I discovered the cancer had returned, and so it was back to chemotherapy and radiation. This time, however, I had the added support from the Crystal People.

I took a favorite crystal point with me to treatment, which helped me to meditate and focus. With the assistance of my crystals, I would enter a sort of Zen state that helped me to endure the unpleasant procedures. I was also literally surrounded by crystals in my bedroom.

Crystals were also effective for the side effects from the treatment. I used a large tabby crystal for nausea. I would rub it on my stomach and the crystal would seem to absorb the disquiet.

Crystal digging kept my mood up, and I continued, even when I had an IV port hanging out of my chest. If my doctors had known I was dragging my port around in the dirt, I'm sure they would have tried to put a stop to the digging. I was quick to figure out that what they didn't know wouldn't hurt them.

Cleaning and sorting was about all I did when I wasn't at the mines picking up more and more crystal. Addiction is not a strong enough word to use. I would often describe it as obsession or craziness, but it was a wonderful kind of craziness.

As I continued to collect more crystal, I was at a loss as to what I was going to do with it. On the phone to my dad in California, I told him about my “what to do with all this crystal” dilemma.

He suggested that I make a website and send the crystal out into the world. Infinite thanks to my dad for suggesting this (and for being my computer guru), it isn't something I would have even considered possible. Thanks, Dad!

Brand new to e-mail, I had no idea how to build a website. In 1995, it wasn't like it is now, where having a website is commonplace.

So what did I do? Using the big yellow HTML for Dummies book, I began learning the basics of Hyper Text Markup Language, aka the language of the Internet, and Arkansas Crystal Works was born.

As I advertise on the website: "Arkansas quartz crystal points and clusters brought to you with respect and honor for the Crystal and Mother Earth." These crystals were never to be marked as "sold," they are marked as "adopted."

Why adoption and not sale? I have never felt that the crystal is "mine" to sell. To me, selling crystal is like selling people. I don't have ownership of the crystal. I am re-homing them as part of the adoption process.

In the beginning, I didn't understand the language of the crystals. I loved them, I felt better around them, but still I couldn't hear their voice; yet, as I handled them, as I looked them over in order to figure out how to describe them to others, I started to notice a difference: this one felt a little more “dense” energetically, this one made me feel giggly inside, and this one felt wise and ancient.

In order to describe each crystal as I was writing the text for the website, I learned more about crystal in general.

I learned how crystal is formed and where it comes from.

I learned what crystal is made of and what its properties are.

In short, I learned what makes crystal, well, crystal, and these are the very topics that we will be discovering next.

How Crystal Forms and Grows

Crystal is made of Silicon dioxide. Silicon dioxide is comprised of one atom of silicon and two atoms of oxygen.

Take a silica rich solution, add 250 million years or so, some heat and pressure, and violà … you have crystal!

It is a daunting task to describe how old crystal really is. The entire existence of humankind is not even a blip on the radar screen in comparison.

I looked at one website in which there was a strip down the side of the page, about as long as a ruler. This "ruler" was made by studying layers of exposed rock. Each *eighth of an inch* represented ONE MILLION years!

There is very little known about the oldest type of rock, which represents about EIGHTY PERCENT of the earth's history. The last twenty percent or so covers a period of something like forty bazillion years.

OK, so I am exaggerating; suffice it to say crystals are ANCIENT beings.

Starting at the most basic level, a crystal molecule is in the shape of a tetrahedron. (A tetrahedron is made up of four equilateral triangles).

Each tetrahedron molecule consists of one atom of silicon and two atoms of oxygen, which is SiO2 or silicon dioxide.

These molecules hook up with each other in a spiral formation. Sometimes the spiral rotates clockwise, sometimes it rotates counter-clockwise. So, when you hold a crystal and the energy feels like it is spiraling one way or the other, it actually is, on a molecular level.

Now we will shift focus from what crystal is made of to where they are formed.

While there are several different ways that mountains are created, the mountains in Arkansas were created by "folding" and "faulting."

To picture this, take a bunch of soft-baked cookies and lay them all out on a cookie sheet. Now take a particularly cranky cookie and push it steadily into all the other cookies.

The cookies that were once flat sort of fold up and pile onto one another. You get some crevasses and cracks and open spaces between your cookies. That's my vision of folding and faulting.

So you have these cookies being piled onto one another by the "cranky" cookie, folding and faulting and pushing up and up. This folding and faulting creates mountains.

Even though the Ouachita Mountains appear to be short and hill-like in comparison to the mountains that shadowed my hometown in California, they are significant in terms of age and erosion.

Bringing your attention from cookies and back to the Earth, the faulting creates cracks in the shale and sandstone.

In many cases, a solution rich in silicon and oxygen fills in the crevasses and cracks.

The silicon and oxygen atoms join, and the resulting molecules start creating quartz crystal.

Given enough room in the crevasses and cracks, the crystals grow into points all along the walls of these spaces, which are now called veins.

After the crystal forms in the veins, clay sediment flows in and acts as sort of a packing material for the crystal. This is the clay you look for when you go crystal digging (you will need to tuck that away in your memory for when we discuss digging later).

Remember the cookies? Shifting and movement from the folding and faulting causes the formed crystal to break and re-growth to occur.

Self-healed crystals are created when crystal breaks off the crystal matrix during Earth movement. They continue to grow over, and, in effect, heal the broken edges.

Shifting back to the big picture, as a mineral, quartz is very common all over the globe. Frequently it is referred to as one of the most common minerals on Earth; that is actually a misrepresentation.

The Earth's crust, that we think of as being so thick and full of minerals, is really nothing more than a skin. So, while it is true that quartz may be one of the most common minerals on the Earth's *surface*, there is a whole lot more "earth" than "surface."

Let's get back to the difference between what we call rock quartz (what we think of as crystal) and quartz the mineral.

Some silicon dioxide doesn't have the room to grow into points, it just sort of fills in the spaces where it can; add in some different mineral atoms and you come up with the other forms of semiprecious gemstones.

With more tight spaces in the earth than wide open veins, *rock* quartz isn't nearly as plentiful as the *mineral* quartz; however, quartz is still quartz vibrationally and on a molecular level.

Whether it is rock quartz, or the squished-in filler form of quartz, it is all silicon dioxide. From here on, however, we're just talking about the "rock quartz" form.

The hardness of a crystal is measured on what is called the Moh's scale. This is a scale that goes from one to ten with softest (number one) being talc and hardest (number ten) being diamond. Quartz ranks in at number seven on the Moh's scale ofhardness.

The clearest crystal is described as “water clear.” When crystals aren't water clear, they are said to have inclusions. A crystal can be included with moisture or air bubbles or other minerals which get trapped inside a crystal during its growth.

When the mineral is just in there, sort of willy-nilly, it is simply called a mineral inclusion. There may be a bit here and a bit there. There might also be a chunk half in and half out.

Phantoms are mineral inclusions formed more evenly throughout the crystal. Phantoms are formed when the crystal is growing, still in solution, and a mineral gets introduced. The forming crystal point is then surrounded by this other mineral. Settling of the mineral causes the solution to return to clear.

To illustrate the settling and subsequent Phantom formation, imagine sitting in your bathtub and dropping mud in your bathwater. Continue lying in your bathtub, deathly still for hours and hours, until the mud settles out of the water and onto you (you are the crystal, the mud is the Phantom).

In a forming crystal, when the solution clears up, the crystal resumes growing, so a "phantom" of the other mineral is trapped within the crystal point. Sometimes this happens several times, with more than one phantom forming inside the resulting crystal point. Mineral inclusions will introduce different energetic properties to your crystal (whether they are freeform or Phantom).

Gas Phantoms and Reverse Phantoms are two other kinds of phantoms which, while they are called Phantom, are different from the type of phantom we have just discussed. In both of these crystals, the phantom occurs just below the surface. Gas Phantoms are discussed more fully, later. Reverse Phantoms are also called Overcoat Quartz and/or Snow Quartz. In these phantoms, the last layer of crystal formed is the phantom, so they appear snowy on the outside and very clear on the inside.

Crystals are also *piezoelectric* (pie-EE-zoh-electric); this simply means that when a crystal is squeezed, it puts of a little bit of electricity. If you slice the crystal at certain angles and then squeeze it, it pulses at different frequencies; so, we can actually say that we are not crazy when we think we feel a vibration because rock crystal actually does have a pulse.

If you have ever looked at the face of your watch and seen the word “Quartz” it means that the watch's tick-tock is powered by a teeny tiny slice of quartz being squeezed by a teeny tiny elf. OK, so maybe it's not being squeezed by an elf, but that movement is caused by quartz and its piezoelectricity. What does that mean about my good ole Grandpappy? It means that the “crazy” guy, sitting on the ground feeling the crystals wasn't nuts, he was onto something!

It feels a little odd for me to be describing my crystal friends in such “just the facts, ma'am” form and function detail, but it is much like when we describe a person anatomically, as in heart, lungs, etc. Describing the physical attributes of the crystal will help us understand the function part of their being later on. We'll be getting to the how-to of connecting with and talking to your crystals soon, though, so hang on!

Shaman, and other wise women and men, throughout the ages have used crystals for vision quests, astral travel, magical workings, and healing. Crystals have been fashioned into tools such as arrowheads and scrapers. They have been polished into skulls, jewelry, mundane and magical tools, for as long as there have been people on the Earth.

In the current age, crystal is also utilized in computers (think Silicon Valley) and in equipment such as oscillators and watches. The crystal that is used in industry is grown in a laboratory to ensure that it is free of impurities.

As mentioned previously, quartz is a prevalent mineral from a global standpoint. Rock quartz can be found as far away as Tibet and China and in the United States, as close as Arkansas, Washington State, Herkimer New York and the Pecos River Valley (which runs through New Mexico and Texas). These are just a few examples; it can be found in *many* more places worldwide.

However, there are only three places where there is enough crystal to actually justify large-scale commercial mining. Those three places are Brazil, Madagascar, and Arkansas.

Arkansas has some of the largest crystal beds in the world. Partially due to the folding and faulting, it was just a great place for them to grow, and grow they did.

Remember what my Crystal Guide, Venus, said earlier, that the Atlanteans seeded this area and that they also placed some of the large Earthkeeper crystals here for safekeeping? From what I have read, and understood, there are colonies of beings tending to the Atlantean crystals inside the Earth.

Knowing that this goes beyond the scope of my personal knowledge, I have asked Venus to speak about this subject for us; she says:

Regarding those whom you call the Blue People, they are an ancient race of beings that have contracted to assist the Crystal People while we live in the Earth. They tend the crystal beds and guard the great Earthkeepers.

Originally they came from the planet you call Sirius; however they have been here (on this planet) for a long, long time.

They live comfortably in the Earth and take their nutrition from the minerals and fluids within.

There are openings where you may see these guards if you are attuned to their energy.

They are a benevolent race of beings and they take their duty as Keepers seriously. We are thankful and grateful for the service they so selflessly provide.

Many thanks to Venus for that information.

The vibration of crystal from Arkansas is described as being different from crystal found elsewhere in the world. I have found the energy to be more clear and immediate.

Thermal waters and magnetic lodestone are two of the reasons that Arkansas crystal is different. Arkansas is a unique place, to be sure; besides the crystal mines, we have the only diamond mine open to the public in North America.

The bulk of the working crystal mines in Arkansas are located in Mount Ida and Jessieville. Let's use Little Rock, as home base, to describe where these places can be found.

If you leave a piece of bread out and a mouse nibbles all along the right side and also takes a bite off the lower left corner, you have the basic shape of Arkansas. Little Rock is in the center.

If you look at a map of Arkansas, you are most likely to see Hot Springs, but not Mount Ida or Jessieville. In traveling on your map southwest of Little Rock to Hot Springs, Mount Ida and Jessieville are north and west of Hot Springs. Drop a blob of jelly on Hot Springs and you are likely to cover Mount Ida and Jessieville in sticky sweetness.

Many of the crystal mines are run by families going back generations; much of the land is leased from the government. With a few exceptions, the mines change hands frequently and the names of the mines often change with the owners.

Damage to the earth and a question of greed has caused some controversy about whether or not mining for the crystals is a good thing or a bad thing. People asked me this question when I first started Arkansas Crystal Works, but I haven't been asked it for many years, so maybe it's not a question in people's minds anymore.

However, since I brought it up, I'll give you my view.

I see it more like a birth. Let me explain.

Crystal Mining (aka "The Birth Process")

Crystals emerge from the earth in two ways; either they are dug out by people, or they surface on their own through natural causes such as folding, faulting and erosion. We've already discussed how long that process takes.

By comparison, when we dig them out, they are "born" via C-Section (versus erosion, which would be natural delivery).

Mother Earth and the Crystal People know how much humanity needs their assistance going into this new era, so they're allowing us to deliver them by C-Section.

To wait for the crystal to emerge on the Earth's time scale, we probably would have destroyed ourselves three or four times over, so that by the time they made their way out into the sunshine, we'd have already been toast. I believe that Mother Earth and the Crystal People are graciously, and intentionally, allowing us to cut open and dig in to pull them out now, while there's still time to save humanity.

Let's get back to the process.

How do the commercial miners know where to begin digging?

In the mines that are already established, they follow the veins and lay of the land; then, depending on the makeup of the ground, and by following clues, they can make an educated guess about where to go next.

Arkansas crystal grows on a matrix in the lining of these crevasses, cracks, and holes in sandstone and shale, so the miners follow the veins.

You might wonder what an Arkansas quartz crystal mine looks like.

I had visions of holes and darkness and large caves full of crystal, something like a dragon's lair in the bottom of a big mountain filled with glistening crystal points.

What the crystal mines in Arkansas *actually* look like is a bunch of red dirt on a mountain top. It is a big hole with a road for driving Earth moving equipment in and out. If the mine is big enough, the road may circle down into the hole (also called the *pit*).

There are big piles of dirt all around the top of this hole, or pit, and trees surround the hole.

It doesn't sound very glamorous, I know. I apologize. I like the dragon's lair image better, too; however, you *are* on the mountaintop, so you can see for miles and miles in every direction.

There are beautiful green trees and rolling hills. The colors in the fall are stunning. It is breathtaking. I could sit on a rock and stare out for hours (or until my rear end goes numb or another crystal beckons, which doesn't usually take more than a few minutes).

Mining typically consists of searching where to dig based on clues given by the strata of the rock, at times blasting with dynamite and then carefully digging out the crystal. The blasting is only done to take away large chunks of rock that can't be dug out with a machine, and it is a very precise skill.

The miners find a good vein and the crystal is harvested by the people who run the mine.

The material that they have blasted, the piles of dirt that they dig out of the way to get to the large veins, is trucked up to the top of the pit and dumped out for people like you and me to dig through. These piles of dirt are called the *tailings*.

There is a lot involved in the process of mining and retrieval of the crystals. Mining is messy, difficult work; it is also careful work.

We have discussed how the mining process compares to birth by C-section. So, too, is it comparable both in the way the babies must be carefully extracted (a cut too deep would not be good for the baby) as well as the relationship to what is termed collateral damage.

Mother Earth is left with scars from the birth process. Trees are sacrificed, and from an aerial view you can locate the mine by seeing a large red scar in the canopy.

In human years, it seems like we have been destructive and careless and Mother Earth has been slashed and scarred forever. However, in Mother Earth years, this scar will heal over, and, like a woman's scar after a C-section, there will be changes in her body, yes, but given time, the scarring fades and is barely noticeable.

Our great Mother is giving birth to Children of Light who have been incubating for millennia. The time has come for them to emerge and assist us into this new era.

I'm so grateful to the Crystal People and to our great Mother for this honor.

We don't want to waste it.

Our role as humans is to help the crystal out of the earth, to be their legs, to get them to where they need to go in order to reach as many people as possible and increase the vibration of all humankind.

We are the transport for them to reach as many places, and people, as we can so they may spread their healing and knowledge and general awesomeness.

The crystals weren't “blessed” with legs. I don't know if that would be a blessing or a curse if they had been. The visual in my mind of crystals running around the place on legs makes me giggle.

On a more serious note, however, they do need our assistance to get to where they need to go so that they can do the most good. This is what I mean about it being time for their birth and delivery. In keeping, our role as Lightworkers is vital.

Crystal has been commercially mined since the early 1900's, but the popularity is increasing exponentially as the vibrations increase into this new era. Their light is needed and we can help. How cool is that?

Small or large, all crystals need a home.

Digging your own crystal is a rewarding and exhilarating experience; because I'll describe digging in much more detail later, for now, I will speak in generalities.

Most of the mines require a small digging fee for the entire day. You simply choose a mine, pay the fee, sign a liability release and then start digging.

Safety is a major concern for all ages. Children need close supervision and must be guided and watched diligently. There are a lot of drop offs and places for little (and big) people to get seriously hurt.

However, if the safety considerations are carefully observed, I would recommend crystal digging to people of all ages. It is important to remember that common sense is the most important tool to use.

A “working mine” will offer the best digging. When choosing a mine, you'll want to find out how often they “work” it. You'll want to know if they dig every day, or if they are digging the day you are going to be there.

Which day will give you the best chance to find something?

Crystal digging is a bit like fishing; a mine that gave you lots of crystal last time may give you very little the next time. It depends on many factors.

It depends on what the mine owners have found in the pit (and subsequently brought up in the tailings).

It also depends on the weather (rain is helpful to wash the dirt off crystals that may not otherwise be seen), and believe it or not, it also depends on your own mood. I have discovered that if I'm not in the right place mentally, the Crystal People seem to go into hiding. When I am feeling good, and my vibrations are high, when I am in a grateful space, I tend to see them more easily.

Don't worry; we will talk more about the specifics of crystal digging later.

Breakage happens quite a lot, as you might imagine. Crystal is hard, but blasting and earthmoving equipment takes its toll. The process creates a lot of loose rock and dirt that has to come out of the pit.

The mine operators are digging for the “premium” crystal, intact large points and clusters, with the key word being intact. The rest comes up in the tailings for rescue by you and me. There is a LOT of “premium” crystal to be found in the tailings; there is also a lot of breakage.

When I say "premium," I am not making a value judgment that these crystals are "premium" because they are "better."

Nor am I saying that the crystals in the tailings aren't as worthy or powerful. In fact, at times, the crystals in the tailings seem more precious to me, because the very act of retrieval is why they *aren't* in one piece.

Mount Ida and Jessieville crystal mines aren't the only place you can find crystal in Arkansas. On hiking trails, along the roadside, even in Lake Ouachita (*Wash*-i-taw), you might happen upon a crystal point or two. Certainly you will find quartz matrix (the smashed-in-the-spaces, non-point kind of quartz crystal we talked about earlier). Of course, finding rock crystal (points) in these places isn't as likely because there is less of it being uncovered by weather and erosion.

Convenience and use play a part in the question of size. Is bigger better? Does a large point put out more energy than a small point?

Certainly, by mass alone, a 500-pound single crystal point is going to exude more energy than a tiny jewelry point, but this is not to say that the smaller points don't have comparable energy or enough energy to matter. Comparatively speaking, a small crystal might have the same energy as a large point.

By example, an ant can move ten to fifty times its body weight. Using that gauge, you can see that ants are stronger than humans, ounce for ounce.

A small point may be stronger than a large point in the same respect; some very small points are deceptively powerful, meaning that bigger in size doesn't always mean better. Also, it is easy to put a small point around your neck or in your pocket. Wheeling a 500-pound crystal around in a wagon would get tiring after a while, don't you think?

Depending on the crystal, its use and your need, a small point can be every bit as helpful to you as its larger cousin. The old adage is true about not judging a book by its cover (or an item by its size).

Understanding all of the mining process is important, but it leads us back to our original question. Are crystals truly sentient beings? What does sentience mean, exactly? According to the Merriam-Webster dictionary, sentience is described as:

- Responsive to, or conscious of, sense impressions
- Aware

I believe that there are many more sentient beings on this Earth than we care to admit. To say the animal kingdom is sentient seems obvious. What about the plant kingdom? What about water? Yes, yes and yes. There have been studies and experiments proving this. Perhaps it's finally time to have someone run a scientific study on crystal.

I would hasten to add that as well as sentient, crystals are also intelligent.

We'll be discussing this in more detail next.

Crystal as Sentient Beings

When you look at crystal, its beauty is obvious; they are sparkly, shiny and gorgeous gemstones.

That is what I initially thought, as I watched the sun flashing off the points and clusters when I was first introduced to them so many years ago.

It simply didn't occur to me that they might have life, that they might also contain an internal spark in addition to the external one that was visible. However, I knew they were special because I could feel their pull.

When I was first learning about crystal and its properties, I read about people who "talked" to their crystal, could hear them speak, and who could feel their vibrations. I was SO jealous!

I thought only *special* people could do it; only those born with a sort of special ability not accessible to regular people like me. I'm guessing, since you are reading this book, that you may also be feeling the same way. This couldn't be further from the truth! Isn't that exciting news?

Both time and experience served to change my opinion.

Initially, for my website, I would describe the crystals from a purely physical perspective: length and width, weight and surface features, the number of sides, faces and edges.

After physically measuring the characteristics of hundreds and hundreds of crystals, I began to notice that I was beginning to receive sensory impressions.

Did this mean that I was finally starting to tune into the special language of the crystals?

It happened slowly.

As I was describing the physical weight, for example, I might also pick up on an energetic weight (lightness or density). Sometimes I felt an overwhelming sense of joy or a silly laughter bubbling up within.

This is when I realized the crystals were speaking to me.

I began to slow down in order to listen to their messages. I started to make a concerted effort to feel their energy in order to decipher their unique form of communication.

You can do this, too! I'm going to teach you.

Actually, you probably already do it; you just haven't been aware that you have been hearing the message, of your crystal, all along.

Stillness is a key feature in the process and following your breath also helps.

It is also important to set preconceptions aside. When you expect a certain thing to happen and it doesn't, you are often disappointed and think you just aren't getting it, that you don't have it and never will.

Your crystals may have been calling to you very strongly, but the chatter in your own mind about what you "should" be experiencing has kept you from hearing them. While you have been desperately seeking that certain "something" that you *expect* to hear or see, you may have completely missed seeing the proverbial forest for the trees.

I found that connecting, stilling myself, clearing my mind and following my breath allowed me to step out of my own way long enough to recognize the signals the crystals were sending.

Since you are already going into this *knowing* that you can do this, you are several steps ahead of where I started!

De-cluttering your space, emptying your mind and being receptive are the key points to learning the language of your crystal. How in the world do we accomplish this?

Unfortunately there is no quick fix. There is no magic box like they have in the movies where the alien's language is automatically translated for humans; no external box, that is!

What's that, you say? There may be a magic box?

Yes, I believe there is.

Located inside each of us, it does require us to figure out what language WE speak in order to translate the language we are trying to understand.

There will be much more on this coming up soon.

Comparing what you sense *before* you pick up the crystal and then *after* you pick it up will help you determine any differences, in other words, signals, signs or "voices."

This is why it is so vital that you check-in with yourself, internally, and also with your external environment before you start.

You will need a baseline, so to speak.

If you aren't familiar with yourself on all levels, physically, emotionally, mentally and spiritually, you won't be able accurately access the language of the crystal.

You need to be able to feel, or sense, the difference and this is crucial. This is also why you need to learn what language you speak.

I believe the crystals are broadcasting on all frequencies; you just need to know which channel comes in most clearly for you. What does this mean?

We've all heard the terms *clairvoyance* and *clairsentience* but what do they mean?

Clair simply means clear.

- Clair*voyance* means clear *seeing*
- Clair*sentienc*e means clear *sensing*
- Clair*audience* means clear *hearing*
- Clair*cognizance* means clear *knowing*

This is what I mean by determining what language you speak.

I always assumed that since I didn't always see auras or didn't see Spirits with my eyes that I didn't have any special senses. I believed that since I wasn't seeing or hearing as my friends did that I didn't have any special "clair" or clear anything! That wasn't true. I now understand that I sense differently than my friends.

Ask yourself these questions: How do I sense? Do I *see* things? Do I *feel* things? Do I *hear* things? Or do I simply *know* things? You must tune into your special sense.

We all have a way we sense other than the obvious, or mundane. I am a "*feeler*." I feel Spirits, I feel energy. I feel emotions and thoughts.

This is the primary way I process the outside information I receive. I also see, but that is secondary to feeling. So I would describe my language as primarily *clairsentient* and then *clairvoyant*. The seeing I do is primarily internal (in my mind's eye).

I have also discovered that the more I work with the Crystal People, the more my sense of Clair*cognizance* is being developed. I simply *know* things.

Seeing stories within your mind's eye, *feeling* pulsing in your body or heaviness in your aura, *hearing* a bell-like tone in your ear are all examples of what information you might receive when listening for the language of your crystal.

It will be different for everyone.

I may pick up a crystal and feel an angelic presence.

I may feel lightness in my body or feel a happiness that wasn't there after initially taking note of my internal sensations (checked-in).

Another person may *see* Angels or lights dancing in the crystal or may simply *know* that there are Angels within that crystal.

These are the different ways we understand the language. This is what I mean when I say that crystals are broadcasting an all wavelengths.

Crystals don't only "show themselves" to seers or "speak" to listeners or "touch" feelers. They are speaking, showing, touching, all senses at all times. It is our job to tune into the clearest channel for us.

We have already determined I am a "feeler," so the descriptions I offer are going to be "feeling" focused. For those of you who speak a different language, simply interject the equivalent term in your language (see, hear, know).

I sometimes sense a heaviness or density in my aura, or on the other side of the spectrum, a giddiness or lightness.

I sense ancient wisdom in some crystals and youthful energy in others.

Holding a certain crystal may touch a great depth of empathy in me.

Sometimes I see stories within my mind's eye. Almost always I feel thrumming, pulsing or vibrations in different areas of my body.

All of these sensations are important to note and wouldn't be possible to differentiate from the norm without the initial baseline check-in that serves to acknowledge what my particular "clair" is (to learn how I process the messages from the crystals).

It is possible to sense animals, birds or even elements in your crystal.

Some crystals have given me the impression of a snowy owl or a baby bird; at other times, a furry animal.

Elements in the form of air or water also present themselves through crystals. Elementals such as Fairies, Deva and as we discussed, Angels may be sensed.

There is SO much knowledge our crystal friends have to tell us; they have lived for so long! Just imagine the stories they have to tell and lessons they have to teach.

Not every crystal is here just to teach, however; they may simply be a companion, here to provide company as you share, and compare, stories.

I think we tend to get into the mindset that because crystals are healers and teachers, and due to their wisdom and age, they are each here for a specific purpose only and not for anything else.

While they may be here for all of these things, they may also have been drawn to you simply to *be*.

Again, preconceptions can cause us to miss the bigger picture.

We have already discussed how bigger in size doesn't necessarily mean better. It is important to remember that small crystals can be every bit as powerful as a large crystal. Speaking in ratios; sometimes a small crystal will emit a greater vibration than a large crystal on a one-to-one basis.

It may vary wildly.

Every crystal is unique. Just like people, there are no two crystals that are the same.

Even chips and chunks of crystal carry energy, healing power and vibration. It's just that their ability to focus energy may not be as effective as a point with a termination; even a point with a damaged tip will still have a basic direction that the energy flows.

In a chunk or point with no discernible top, bottom or sides, you would expect the energy to be more diffuse, radiating from all directions. There will be less focus, but they are energetically still very powerful and useful. Depth, wisdom and healing properties aren't relegated solely to crystals without dings or mine damage.

Crystals are also categorized as being “old souls” or “new souls.” This is sort of a misnomer, as they are ALL old souls in comparison to humans; however, they *do* emit different feelings of age.

Some emanate a newer, younger, more mischievous or playful vibration. On the other hand, some feel wise and very old, like your great-grandmother might seem.

They may seem quiet, gentle, deeply still, full of wisdom and lore, but less apt to be jumping around and playing games.

Old soul crystals are likely to have what are called Barnacles on them.

Barnacles are described as small crystal points that are attached to a larger point (or cluster). Typically they tend to be on one side of a crystal (a bit like moss on a tree grows primarily on one side, not all the way around).

Sometimes there are so many Barnacles they appear to be encrusted with jewels.

The energy of these crust-like Barnacles is glittery, shiny and joyous.

It is a wonderful contrast to the ancient deep wisdom which comes from the old soul crystal to which they are attached.

Not every "old soul" crystal has Barnacles and not every crystal with Barnacles emits "old soul" energy. It's important not to have preconceptions, remember? These are just guidelines to get you started.

A proper introduction is the best first step in the process of getting to know the Crystal People.

Most books describe the nuts and bolts of their "anatomy" if you will, with no discussion of asking permission, shaking hands and becoming acquainted.

I liken it to walking up to a person and flipping up their skirt to see what's under there.

Imagine doing this with a professor, doctor, shaman or someone's great-great-grandmother! It's unthinkable, right?

It's the same with our crystal friends.

If you haven't made the proper introduction, it's just not cool to snatch one up and start examining surface features, facets, terminations and body type, and then toss it back down on the table if it doesn't have the features you're looking for.

It is a common mistake and our crystal friends ultimately forgive our ignorance. However, now that we have the knowledge that there is a protocol to introductions and becoming acquainted, then I think it's polite to follow it.

As discussed earlier, it goes back to the fact that these great beings aren't simply tools to be picked up and utilized without a proper connection.

When I think of the way we have been previously taught to select a crystal simply as a tool to be used, I have a visual in my mind's eye of rifling through a toolbox, tossing hammers and wrenches about, indiscriminately.

You might look at a hammer and judging by its weight and size decide whether or not it seems sufficient for the job at hand. While judging a tool by its looks may be appropriate, it is not recommended with a potential new healer, teacher or friend.

Ignorance is the typical reason most of us have been guilty of unashamedly looking up the skirts of our crystal friends.

We didn't do it out of arrogance or maliciousness. I envision the comparison to the actions of a two-year-old versus that of an adult. That is why I am sure they continue to excuse our crude manners; we simply didn't know.

I now want to share the protocol that I feel is necessary, so that we can all be as respectful as possible.

It doesn't have to take a lot of time; it can be as quick as a thought.

- *Establish* a heart connection
- *Ask* permission
- *Erase* preconceptions
- and then *connect*

Listen to the wisdom of your elders; express your gratitude and thankfulness to these ancient beings who have allowed us to cut them away from their Mother so that they may be of service to all sentient beings living on the planet.

I'm sure you will hear this from me again, but it is not unusual for me to kiss my crystal friends, rub them on my cheek, and hold them close to my heart.

I have come home from the crystal mine, many times, with mud on my lips and grit in my teeth. I consider myself lucky to have been given the opportunity to kiss an ancient being.

Let's talk next about our role as Lightworkers and how our Guides and Angels figure into the overall equation.

Lightworkers, Angels and Spirit Guides

Lightworkers are healers, masters and servants of humanity who have contracted to come back at this time, when they know they can be of the most service.

They come in all shapes and sizes, with many different skill sets and areas of expertise, with the common goal of service; service to mankind, service to the Earth and all of her many inhabitants.

It's not an easy task for which we have signedup.

While many of us have had difficult life experiences as part of our path, our learning, it has all been a necessary part of the greater plan.

We are beginning to awaken to our purpose now, during this time of great change, as the new era begins.

It is both a scary and exciting time we are in.

Soul contracts, both individual and as a group, are what we are playing out.

Look to your fellow Lightworkers, take their hands and know that together we can do anything!

According to the Maya, Hopi and other indigenous peoples, with tradition passed on from generation to generation, this is the end of a cycle 28 thousand years long.

This knowledge and these stories have been passed, hand to hand, not unlike the continuity of knowledge within the Crystal People.

While humankind has not spanned the eons encompassed by the life of the crystals, we have lived well into the thousands of lifetimes.

Most of humanity's knowledge, however, is broken up as memories that have been made, and forgotten, over and over again, but our souls have not forgotten. Humanity's collective consciousness has held this knowledge safe for all of us.

It is into this that we are tapping during the birth of this new era.

With the help of our crystal friends, Angels and Guides, we will raise the vibration of the planet. It is our responsibility to help increase and then to maintain the increased vibration that will be required for a successful completion of this cycle, thereby leading into the beginning of the next.

Ancient civilizations such as Atlantis and Lemuria figure into our current era. That seems quite a stretch to some of us.

How does the ancient past connect with us now?

Time outside the duality of our human experience is not linear; everything is happening now. How do the crystals, and ourselves, fit into this linear timeline?

Most of us view time like a yardstick laid out on a table.

Today might be at 10 inches and tomorrow at 11 inches. The past is "behind us," from 9 inches and back.

I believe that time is actually flowing in a continuum; not forward and back, but more up and down. Turn the yardstick on end, and everything is happening now.

This non-linear construct can be mind-blowing!

While I believe this is how it works, I sometimes can't quite wrap my head around it, logically. How can past, present and future all be occurring at the same time?

To those of us that have been taught that time is always, and only, linear, considering the possibility of an “eternal now” can be monumentally confusing!

The ancient “you” who is living in Atlantis also exists now. The lifetimes we believe are in our ancient past are actually occurring right now.

It's as if our lifetimes are written on sheets of paper and they are all stacked, one on top of the other, rather than laid out side-by-side, marching along like inches on the yardstick.

This mind-warp is too confusing to maintain while living our day-to-day lives, so we have chosen to pretend as if the inches on the yardstick, or pages from the stack, are laid out side-by-side.

That is SO much easier for us to understand.

If you can maintain the thought that everything is happening now, that is enough. You don't have to know how, or be able to visualize it, or even understand it.

Suffice it to say, it simply IS.

If this resonates as true for you, then you may agree. If it does not, then simply disregard. As with all the ideas I present as true for me, if it doesn't resonate as true for you, toss it out by the wayside.

Continuing to talk in terms of time as being stacked in one paper pile will be too confusing, so for the ease of the discussion, I'm going to go with our common notion of the page-after-page, inch-after-inch scenario; time marching steadily onto the right, leaving the past behind us to the left.

Ancient civilizations are behind us, future civilizations are yet to come.

Viewing time in this way, we can see how the crystals might serve as a thread from the ancient past to the present and into the future.

Having such incredibly long life spans, they are able to embody the “paper in a stack” version of time.

The crystal you may be holding right now was physically present throughout the ancient past, is with you now in this current moment, and will continue to exist into the distant future.

It is the same way that I view our souls, but adding a physical body component is what trips us up in understanding such a concept.

Feel free to use the lifetime of the crystal to help you visualize.

Even though we may need to keep with the flat yardstick or paper side-by-side construct, the crystals can work as our anchor. Through them, we can access the past, present and future right here in our hand. How cool is that?

Along with memory, we can tap into ancient or future healing, amplification of thought, energy and vibration, all in this NOW moment.

If healing is present either in our past or our future, we can access that through crystals in the *Now*.

They are portals.

It's not an easy task, to be sure, to acknowledge an "Eternal Now," but viewing crystal in its proper state as sentient beings will help us in this task.

Experience is a great teacher. Who better a teacher than someone who has been around millennia longer than we have?

We can tap into the wisdom and knowledge of these ancient beings and use their memory and experience to help us in the present moment.

They have instant access to the timeline as upright. They understand the challenges we so often encounter as we strive for full awareness, and they are willing and happy to lend us their assistance.

All we need to do is acknowledge their wisdom, while being grateful, thankful and respectful.

Crystal assistance can come in many forms; assistance with things of a technical nature (knowledge), assistance with healing or physical needs (comfort), and assistance with our emotions (companionship).

In this way, crystals make great friends.

We go to our human and animal friends for all these things, do we not? Our crystal friends are here to help us in this same manner, as well.

Different crystals help in different ways, just like human friends and acquaintances.

Some crystals will serve as our healers; some will help boost our energy and give us motivation; some we can go to like a trusted grandparent, for comfort and advice, and some are just fun pals to hang out with.

Different realms, other than past and future, may also be accessed through the assistance of our crystal friends. There are the astral realms, dream realms, even elemental realms. Certain crystals are helpful in accessing the astral plane. Faden quartz is one of these. With a line in them similar to the silver cord, they are helpful in astral projection and travel.

Dreaming can be enhanced with the assistance of crystals.

Properly programmed, crystals can help us with lucid dreaming and dream recall.

Certain crystals have connections with the elemental realms. They may have access to fairies and other elementals. The physical elements of air, fire, water and earth are also accessible. Both Devic crystals with Fairy Frost as well as Rainbow crystals are good for this purpose.

While these are merely basic generalities, it is still helpful to have a basic idea of the type of crystal to seek when looking for assistance in a specific area.

Spirit Guides may be contacted with the assistance of our crystal friends. A request for that connection, openness and meditation can also help with this. Until we are able to still our minds and calm the chatter, we may not hear what our Guides have been telling us. Spirit Guides aren't going to yell, scream or stomp their feet; this isn't the way they communicate. Until we get quiet and listen, we aren't going to hear them.

Our crystal friends know this, and so if we ask, they will work hard to help us quiet our minds and hear the whispers from within our souls. Not only can our crystal friends be very helpful with focus, they can also amplify our desire to connect with our Guides.

A dear friend of mine channels Spirit Guides. I met her though my association with the Crystal People. She has helped me to re-establish and strengthen my connection with my own Spirit Guides.

I have learned, through her channeled information, that daily meditation will deepen our connection, and, subsequently, our ability to hear our Guides when they speak. When you get used to the energy of your Spirit Guides in a meditative state, you will be better able to access their energy and recognize their loving "voices" when you are busy. Having a crystal friend dedicated to assisting you with this task may help you maintain your focus during these daily meditations.

This increase in awareness of the voice of our Spirit Guides is the same as our increase in awareness of the voice of our crystal friends.

Much of this book is being written with the help of my dear crystal Guide, Venus. As a result, a heartfelt "thank you" has to be extended to both my friend, Angel, for helping me connect, and to Venus for guiding me with information.

Our crystal friends can assist us in many ways. Besides helping us directly with issues, such as focus and connection, they can also lead us to people, places and situations that will serve to further enhance our learning and spiritual growth.

Many of my dearest friends were brought to me this way.

Angels may also be contacted through the assistance of our crystal friends. Some crystals have an angelic presence. Whether there are Angels in the crystals, or the crystal is able to bring through angelic energy because it has come in contact with Angels, or whether they just vibrate on the same frequency as Angels, I'm really not sure. Suffice it to say that they are there, accessible through our crystal friends.

I have yet another wonderful friend whom I met through my contact with the Crystal People. She is a very angelic being herself. I sent a small cluster to this friend of mine as a thank you gift (I always send a gift of thanks with my crystals that I adopt out) simply because I was led to it and felt “this is the crystal for Renee!”

When she received it, she turned it over, and there on the back, in the matrix of the cluster, were two flying Angels.

I didn't go looking for a crystal with Angels. I felt a

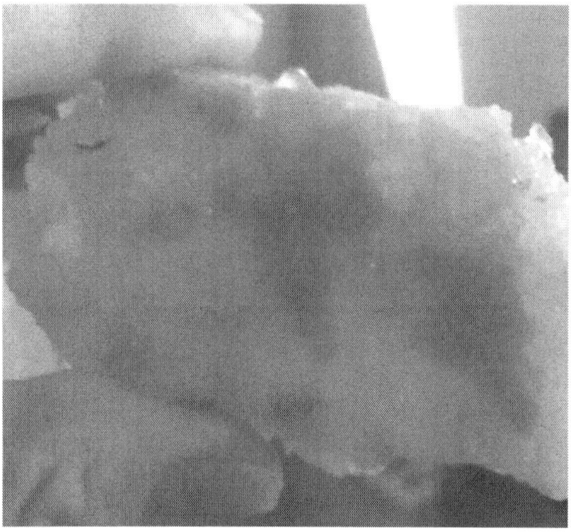

vibration and a call that said "*Hey! I am here for Renee! Send me!*" and sure enough, there were Angels. It was amazing. Man, oh man, I love crystals!

Stories pour in through my adoption of the crystals, including those of Angels, Spirit Guides and elementals.

Another area I hear about frequently is the way crystals are able to interact with our pets.

Cats and dogs react to crystals in different ways. My friend Renee has a bowl of crystals that her cat likes to touch. It uses its little paw and moves them gently here to there.

Many people talk about their cats climbing into the box in which the crystal was shipped. Upon the arrival of the crystal to their new home, I have also heard stories where both cats and dogs will immediately pick them up in their mouths and carry them off.

Crystals are also great to use for pet therapy in healing, protection and energy. I have sewn crystals onto the collar of my little Chihuahua friend, Ody (the crystal digger).

You can place them in, and around, their pet beds; even in their water bowls.

There are two things to consider if you decide to do this.

Number one: make sure the crystal is large enough that your pet isn't going to accidentally ingest it, especially large dogs with small crystals. Obviously small dogs aren't as likely to lap up a larger crystal.

Number two: make sure that the crystals are clean of any acid residue that may be present from the cleaning process. For safety's sake, setting the crystal *near* rather than *in* the bowl is a better idea.

Speaking of acid and the cleaning process leads me to another great way to work with our crystal friends. What about crystal in drinking water, water for our plants or even for our pet fish?

Crystal can be a beautiful and healthy addition to a fish tank. You need to beware, however, that crystal is often cleaned with oxalic acid, making it pretty and rust free. If you're putting crystal into drinking water, or into a fish tank, be sure to use crystal that has been cleaned with water only (no acid). In a fish tank, I would even be wary of using soap.

Please don't drop a newly acquired crystal, or cluster, into your fish tank thinking you will be helping your fish with the healing properties of quartz (which would be a great idea) if you are using crystal which may have residual bits of acid on it (which would NOT be a great idea).

The same goes for your own drinking water.

If it is a single point that doesn't have a lot of crevasses, I would think that a crystal previously cleaned in acid would be safe to use if you cleansed it with a brush and rinsed it very well before putting it into your drinking water.

However, a better alternative is to place the crystal near, but not into, the water. This is the safest bet, especially where our fish friends are concerned.

Placing a crystal near your drinking water, especially if you program that crystal for a specific intent, such as health, energy, etc., will help to raise the water's vibration.

Plants and trees also benefit from crystal. You can put crystal into your watering container for indoor plants.

I have also buried crystal points and chunks around the base of a plant to help increase its growth and energy.

Clusters placed around the base of trees are helpful energetically; besides being beautiful to look at, the crystals also draw fairies and elementals to your trees.

You may hang crystals in your trees for your own pleasure, to attract fairies and elementals and also for the tree spirit itself. We'll talk more about this later.

We have determined that crystals help us to access Spirit Guides, Angels and Elementals, as well as to connect with our animal and plant friends.

I believe that crystal naturally speaks the language of each of these beings.

Remember what I said earlier about crystal broadcasting on many different channels in many different languages?

It doesn't just apply to the different ways humans understand, but exactly how do we go about learning to speak to them?

That's next!

Connecting With Your Crystal

Selecting which crystal with which to connect is the first step in connecting. If you haven't chosen a crystal friend, then how can you bond, right?

The selection process can happen in many different ways. It may be as simple as you seeking a specific type of crystal.

As in the example we used before, perhaps you want assistance with astral travel, so you decide that you want to find a Faden crystal.

The search may well *begin* there, but while you are looking for that crystal, you may be drawn to an entirely different type.

You may see a picture of one on the internet, or you may find a crystal at a local store. It might not be a Faden, but it is possible, and, actually it is quite likely, that the crystal to which you are drawn wants to help you with your goal.

If you have it in your mind that you want help in a specific area, then often the crystal that can offer that help will present itself to you.

You may not have a specific desire, but if you are open to the blessings crystals can bring into your life, the right crystal will be drawn to you, or rather, will draw you to it.

You may dream of a crystal and begin your search based on what you dreamed (for example, the basic size, shape, color, etc).

These are all valid ways of selecting.

You may believe that you are choosing the crystal, but in reality, the crystal is choosing you.

I also offer this type of service; if you are looking for a particular crystal, I can listen to the crystals that currently live with me to see which one wants to come work with you.

Once you have your crystal in hand, be sure to introduce yourself. It doesn't have to be what you think of as a lengthy, formal introduction. It's more of an energy exchange which can occur in milliseconds.

Ask the crystal if it is the one you should be working with. You should get a reaction; personally, I feel it in my gut.

My friend, Angel, whose primary “clairs” are clair*audience* and clair*voyance*, often hears a verbal response in much the same way she does when she channels Spirit Guides.

Your reaction may be entirely different, depending on how you most clearly connect with Spirit (your own personal “clair”).

If you have no response, either from the crystal, or internally, I would say it is a no.

But let's say it is a yes. What's

next?

Assume you've made your initial introduction in a store and you decide that you both connect. This initial exchange doesn't have to be long or extensive. If you have a heart connection, you will know.

Once you get your crystal home, I encourage you to proceed as follows, beginning with posture.

Use any meditative posture that works for you. I suggest having both feet flat on the floor, and your spine straight.

I find if I have my feet down and my head up it works best. It connects me to both Heaven and Earth.

Leaving your crystal on a surface in front of you, clear your mind and do an initial check-in with your body.

Close your eyes and notice what your body feels like.

Does it feel heavy or light?

Do you have pain anywhere?

Is your mind blank and clear?

Once you are sure about your body, it is time for you to make your more formal acquaintance with your new crystal friend.

Pick up your crystal. Experimentation with different grips and positions will show you the way the crystal wishes to be held.

Hold it in one hand to see if it feels comfortable there.

Try the other hand.

Hold it with the termination facing away from you and then towards you.

Usually the crystal will have a preference. This may either be due to surface features or the way the energy spirals, clockwise or counterclockwise.

Experiment with different grips. Try holding it firmly and then loosely.

You may be drawn to hold your other hand over the top of the crystal.

All of these positions are trials. You don't have to try to figure out on your own what the crystal prefers; let it tell you. You will be able to sense what is right and what is not right for that particular crystal.

All of this will only be possible if you clear your mind and get rid of any preconceived ideas of what to expect.

Notice any reaction you have.

You have already cleared your mind, so you should be a blank slate now. Check in again with yourself.

What do you feel physically that is different than how you felt before you picked up the crystal?

Do you feel lighter or heavier (denser)?

If you had any pains or aches, are they still there?

If they are, are they different in any way?

Do you feel any pulsing, throbbing or vibrations?

Moving into non-physical reactions, clear your once mind again.

If you take a deep breath and center, it will help.

Feel your feet on the floor and sink into your feelings.

Connect with your crystal mentally now.

What do you feel?

Are you experiencing a different emotion than before you held your crystal?

Do you feel mentally lighter or denser?

I sometimes experience contentment or even sadness within me that wasn't present before.

You may sense stories or see visions. There may be a light inside your mind's eye that wasn't present before.

You may feel a deep knowing or wisdom.

You may get an impression of age (youthful play or ancient knowing).

You may sense a predominantly masculine or feminine energy, or a mixture of both.

All of these are possible sensations you may have, and all of them are because your crystal is talking to you.

Depending on your personal "language" style, your answers will be formatted in sights, sounds, feelings, or knowing. The sensations are limitless.

Be sure to spend as much time as you like for this; remember, you are connecting with your new friend.

Information may be coming to you, but your next question (which was always mine when I began) might be, "Is this the crystal speaking to me, my higher Self, a Spirit Guide or is it just my imagination?"

Sometimes I still get hung up on, "Whom exactly am I speaking with? Am I just crazy and it's all in my head? Is it just me making this up?"

The answer to all those questions is yes! It IS in your head, and if we all are one, then no matter who it is, it *is* "just you" talking to yourself.

The truth is, if it is good information, if it is positive, and if you find it helpful, it really doesn't matter *where* it is coming from. This is advice I continue to give myself, as well.

If the sensations or information you perceive is negative or not helpful, you can be sure that it isn't from the higher realms (the higher realms would be your higher Self, your Guides or Angels, or the Crystal Being itself); so you *can* determine who is NOT speaking to you. If it is positive and helpful, then good deal; it may be any and all of the above-mentioned high-vibrational entities.

If it is a negative thought or feeling, or of an obviously lower vibration, then it could possibly be your ego (that little part inside each of us that is judgmental and sometimes a little bit cranky).

You also may be picking up residual energy from your environment or accessing unresolved emotions within yourself which you didn't clear before beginning.

You can be sure it is not a lower level *entity*.

How can you be sure of this? Crystals are never going to channel low vibrations from a negative entity through to you. When darkness is present and you turn on a light, the dark is always replaced by light.

You should feel a shift in your vibration from the beginning of your introductory session (talk, visit, whatever you want to call it) with your new friend.

Enjoy the time you spend with your crystal. Notice any physical differences you may feel. Thank your crystal for spending the time with you.

I always feel a heart connection with each crystal, knowing that I have just made another life-long friend.

Put your crystal wherever it is you want or feel led to (pocket, shelf, bedside, etc) and reconnect periodically.

Clear your energy field and ground yourself.

Connect with your crystal, even if it is just when walking by, or bring your crystal into your mind and say hello. We'll call this process a "touch-in" which leads me to the next topic, which is an exciting one!

Experience has taught me that I can, indeed, maintain a relationship with my crystals, even from a very long distance. Once you have made that connection, you can tap into (revisit) that crystal's energy.

I maintain a connection with all the crystals I adopt out or re-home.

I am creating a connection with them when I sit down to get to know them in order to introduce them to you on the website. I tap in emotionally and mentally, as well as physically. The crystal and I create that connection together.

Almost like the silver cord that connects our astral body to our physical, a sort of etheric cord is created between you and your crystal friend.

Once you have created that bridge between you and the crystal, all you have to do is imagine that crystal and follow the cord to it.

Intent is paramount.

If you intend to make a solid and lasting connection with your crystal, then you will.

If you request, during your visit, that you and your crystal friend make a connection that will be maintained even when you aren't in touch physically, and believe that this has occurred, it has!

Initially, you may not feel it, but if you believe that you have an etheric cord attached (which indeed you do), it will be easier to access it. If at first you don't feel the cord, just trust that you have this connection and that with experience, you will soon be able to sense the bond.

First practice saying hello to your crystal friend from another room, and then try accessing it for more complex tasks such as healing or communication.

I would begin with a simple hello (an astral hug, if you will). In time, you will build up your ability to do more and more.

I am able to access crystals all over the planet, even with crystals I haven't yet "met" in this lifetime. It is possible, believe me.

Twenty years ago, I never would have believed I could do this. You can do it, too! Start with baby steps and before long you will be running a marathon!

Gratitude is a really good place to start. Be thankful to your new crystal friend for its willingness to make a connection with you.

After you have mastered long-distance hellos and hugs, which are comparable to walking and jogging, you might want to try something more complex. Try talking with your crystal or asking it for healing energy or an increase in your vibration. This would be comparable to running a 5K.

When you are ready to take this next step, start by imagining your connecting cord.

If you have trouble getting to your crystal with your mind, try visualizing it like a kids' old-fashioned tin-can telephone, the crystal being one “can” and you being the other, each connected by your etheric cord (the string).

You may be very good at visualization and you might not need a mental prompter at all. Do whatever works for you with your "clair" (your style of sensing).

Mood elevation is one thing you may experience when you access your crystal.

Crystals vibrate at a very high frequency, remember, so when you connect to that higher vibration, your internal vibration wants to level up to match.

It's a bit like water in a glass; if you ping a crystal glass full of water, and there are a bunch of other glasses of water around it, all the water will start rippling at the same frequency.

Examples of sensations you may experience with just a brief "touch-in" with your crystal include feeling a sparkling energy or simply a relief from a burden that has been weighing you down.

Longer periods of meditation and focused connection will obviously reap more benefits than a quick touch-in made while you're doing something else.

Once you are accustomed to connecting at shorter distances, longer distances will be possible. This would be comparable to stepping up from the 5-K to a half-marathon, then to a full marathon scenario.

Familiarize yourself energetically with short touch-ins (hugs and hellos), followed by practicing more sustained connections through meditation and focused attention on connecting, either in the same room or from another room.

When you are just beginning, I would initially suggest keeping the distance between you and your crystal within your house.

As you practice, you will find that there is no limit to the distance you can span.

Connecting with your crystal energetically is a bit like talking on a phone. You can be talking with your friend right next door or three states away. Once the connection is made, it doesn't matter how far away you are, it still feels like your friend is right next to you.

After you have mastered connecting with your crystals for yourself, you can work on accessing the energy of your crystal, requesting that it go to another person for emergency healing or assistance. I do this often. It is an advanced technique, but with time and practice I know you will be able to do it, too!

Closing the connection you've established with your crystal friend is an important final step.

You don't want to just drop your "can" and run off to something else while your crystal friend is still hanging onto her "can." Imagine a phone conversation. Everyone has experienced being on the phone only to find out the person at the other end has dropped the connection, which isn't fun for the person left holding the phone.

Closing the connection (setting down the can) doesn't mean that you are cutting the string and the connection is permanently severed. Once you've made the connection, it is solid. It *is* polite, though, to indicate when the conversation is complete.

It's as easy as ending a phone call. Being thankful and grateful to your crystal friend for the conversation and saying "see you later" is all that is required.

Once you are finished, ground yourself. Remember, you are accessing higher vibrations so you might feel spacey or ungrounded afterwards. It is wise to ground out that energy with whatever method works best for you.

Clear your energy field with breath; feel the earth beneath you.

If it has been a long "conversation", you may need to eat something or go for a walk. Use your favorite method of grounding.

Connecting and making friends has been the topic for quite awhile now.

Remember how we talked about it being important to make a connection before whipping up the skirt of your friend to see what's under there?

It is perfectly okay to go ahead and take a physical look at your crystal after you have had your initial heart connection or introduction. You don't have to spend hours and hours before looking at your crystals' physical characteristics.

If you are in a store, for example, there simply isn't time for the kind of bonding we just discussed. Your initial connection may be as quick as a handshake or hug.

Once you have established that you want to be friends and made the initial heart connection (which may only take seconds), it is fine to look at your crystal's physical characteristics.

This is where it is handy to understand a little bit about the anatomy of your crystal, so, let's take a look under that skirt, together, shall we?

Crystal points are hexagonal, so all rock quartz has six sides. While there are exceptions to this rule (a few examples are Elestial crystals and joined crystals), you can depend on rock quartz crystals to have six sides to the body of the point.

Remember we said that crystal grows on a matrix. To picture this, imagine a hand; the palm would be similar to the matrix with the fingers resembling the crystal points. Smoosh a whole BUNCH of hands together palm to palm and you would have a cluster.

There are some crystals that don't grow on a matrix, they basically grow from a 'seed' of silicon dioxide in clay, but we'll take the time right now only to discuss clusters with a matrix for the sake of not making your brain explode.

The points of a cluster aren't all going to grow out of the matrix straight up like fingers on a hand. In playing “this is the church and this is the steeple” with your hands (join hands and interlace your fingers), you will see that this is a more accurate picture of a cluster made of palms and fingers. Some will lay sideways and others upright; some are larger and some smaller. The cluster has been forming for millennia, so as the earth moves, the direction of the original matrix may shift and points may fill in the gaps; it really is a veritable hodgepodge of crystal growing excitement!

Breaking and subsequent healing (or re-growth) occurs frequently in the lifetime of a crystal. Remember the folding and faulting that created the mountains in Arkansas? Well, this movement continues. Over the lifetime (millennia) of the crystal, the movement of the Earth, both in the form of normal continental drift, as well as earthquakes and seismic activity, will cause previously formed crystal to break.

If there is still a solution of silica and oxygen, as well as heat and pressure present, the crystal will continue to grow.

Sometimes a crystal will be sheared in half and will appear to be glued back together. This is what is referred to as re-growth and self-healing.

Crystals growing adjacent to each other, in clusters, often will not grow together (stick to each other) and when the movement occurs and the crystals are broken off the matrix, they will be left with an imprint of the other crystal (or crystals) which they grew next to. While I've never seen these referred to, or described in any book, to date, I call them Imprints. The picture at the beginning of this chapter has a large crystal Imprint.

Typically, a crystal point will have one end that is "up." Again, there are exceptions, but for our purposes, and until I indicate otherwise, we're just going to talk about what we think of as a typical single crystal point.

When you pick up a crystal, it will have an orientation: up, down, front and back. I always took it for granted that everyone knew this, but it might not be as obvious as I once thought. The top of the crystal is the end with the facets and the base, typically, is the more flat end; the body of the crystal is the part between the base and the top.

Remember we discussed the body will have six sides. Crystal points are basically like a cylinder with six walls or sides. Each of the six sides doesn't have to be the same size and most often they are not. Sometimes one of the sides is so narrow you might miss it in your original count, making you think you have a point with only four or five sides. As before, so, too, there are exceptions to this six-sided rule, which we will talk about later.

As a means of comparison, if you look at a number two pencil (the yellow kind we used in school), you will see that it is six-sided. Comparing a crystal to a pencil, the non-sharpened end would be the base of the point where it was attached to the matrix and the sharpened end would be the top (or termination). If you were to sharpen your pencil with a knife, making one cut per side, you would then have a proper pencil-to-crystal comparison.

Growth of a point will usually cause horizontal striations on the sides called lineation. Sometimes these striations are very pronounced and deep, sometimes they are barely visible.

These striations are a good starting point if you have an atypical crystal and are having trouble determining top from bottom and sides from faces. Examples of atypical crystals would include Elestial crystals, crystals which are only partially complete (such as pieces of crystals or broken points) or crystals with many Imprints.

Begin by looking for the parts of the crystal which have horizontal striations. Those are the sides. Now you have an orientation to your crystal and you can proceed from there.

Lineation on some points can be used like a zipper. If you drag your thumbnail down the side of a point with deep striations, you are "unzipping" the crystal. Unzipping enables you to access information within the crystal.

To zip it back up, turn the point upside down (point down) and drag your thumb from the base to the tip (you're still zipping from top to bottom directionally). While it seems silly to flip the crystal on its head to zip up its zipper; the top-to-bottom zipping action feels more consistent and deliberate. I have always turned the point upside down and moved my thumb from north to south. You do what works for you.

I have not personally noticed anything immediately spectacular happen when I "unzip" a crystal; I do notice a slight “opening” or deeper access, but it isn't startling or pronounced, it seems to be more general. I don't think it is absolutely necessary (meaning I don't think you will be unable to connect with the information inside your crystal if you don't unzip it), but is possible that you can access deeper levels of information by doing so. Try it out and see what works best for you!

If a point has no striations on any of the sides at all, you can almost guarantee it is a point that has been polished mechanically. Polished points are still just as useful and powerful; you simply can't read surface features because they have been ground away.

Sometimes crystal is polished because of surface dings or marring caused from the mining process. Lots of Brazilian points come to us completely polished (termination, bottom, and sides). Almost always they are also polished with a flat, beveled base. More often than not, if the sides are polished, the termination will be polished, too, but this isn't always the case. At times just one side or face (as well as the base) will be polished while the rest of the crystal is left in its natural state.

Many times a point will be polished into a Merlin or Generator (six equal faces with a centrally located point) or even Channeler or Dow. However, while the termination may have been ground or polished *externally* into that shape, the *internal* structure is still going to have the energy of the configuration prior to the polishing.

To demonstrate, let's take a look. Grasp the crystal around the body, turn the crystal and look straight down into the termination of the point. Imagine it as a clock face. In a Generator/Merlin or a Dow crystal, for example, all the faces will come together in the center and the tip of the crystal will be in the very center of the clock face.

Let's imagine a crystal which *isn't* a Generator/Merlin or Dow which has its tip or termination leaning over to, say, three o'clock. As we know, the energy of the crystal will spiral up the body and out the tip.

In this non-centrally located termination example, internally, this crystal is spiraling up and out the side of the termination (rather than the center). If this “three o'clock” oriented crystal were artificially polished or ground into the shape of a Generator or Dow configuration (tip in the center of the clock face), the energy won't be as intensely focused out the center as a crystal which occurred in that configuration naturally. That is the reason people sometimes say that polished crystals aren't as “powerful” as natural crystals.

In truth, what they are feeling is the discrepancy between the directional flow the artificially polished termination *indicates* the energy is going and the flow it *actually* has, determined by the internal molecular structure.

Returning to the basic anatomical structure discussion, the point or end of the crystal is called the termination. It is confusing to refer to a single crystal as a “point” and to also call the end of a single crystal the “point,” so we call the top, or end, a *termination*.

The base is the opposite end from the termination.

Some crystals have two terminations (one on each end) and these are called Double Terminated crystals.

Some crystals have multiple terminations such as Extra Terrestrial crystals which have a single termination at the top and many large terminations at the bottom. Sometimes Extra Terrestrial crystals (or ETs) are referred to as Extra Termination crystals (a different take in the initials ET). I prefer the name Extra Terrestrial. ET crystals have a space-like energy, and visually, the name also fits (imagine a rocket ship with flames coming out the bottom).

Looking at the base, if a crystal breaks off the matrix during the mining process, it will look like broken glass. When crystal breaks, it has a curved shape that is called conchoidal (shell shaped). However, if the crystal broke off while it was still in the earth, during the growth process, it may be in any stage of self-healing.

To begin, look at the base to see if it looks obviously broken (like glass). If it doesn't, it may simply seem a little smoothed over or almost sandblasted. If it looks like this (smoothed over), it hasn't been recently broken, but neither is it self-healed.

It may have tiny triangles, like scales, sealing over the end. This is the look of a crystal that is self-healed. The self-healing may be as small as tiny scales that are only visible if you tip it to the light source (more on that later) or the triangles may be large, almost like layers of faces. They will all be parallel to each other and lying at an angle like scales if it is self-healed.

Bases aren't the only place you will find these characteristic triangular layered shapes of self-healing. Sides, or even faces, may be self-healed. Occasionally large areas on clusters are self-healed where points broke off during their growth.

Back up to the top of the point, the termination is further divided into what are called facets or faces. Let's call them faces instead of facets from here on out. Each of the six sides (walls) will have one face (roof). A typical crystal point will have six sides on the body and six faces on the terminating end. The faces are what make up the pointy end of the crystal.

There will be what is called a "main face" which is usually the largest face of the point. In order to determine the front of the crystal from the back, simply find the main face; that is the front. In some points you will find three main faces (a Dow crystal) or two main faces (a Transmitter crystal), but we will discuss this later.

Start counting faces by putting your finger on the main face and count until you make your way back around to the face under your finger. If you count more than six faces in the termination, then you have a Window (or more than one Window depending on the number of faces over six). If, when you count your faces, there are only six, then none of them is a Window.

Many times a face will have the *appearance* of a Window (for example, it may seem to be diamond-shaped or even appear to be "floating" between a side and the termination) but don't let this mislead you. Always begin by counting faces, and if there are only six, it is not a Window.

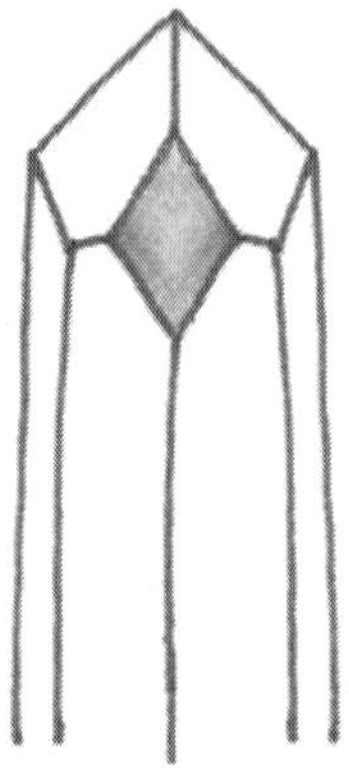

When you discover that you do indeed have more than six faces, in order to determine which ones are the *extra* faces, (Windows), start at the top of each side of the crystal and find its corresponding face, or roof. When you find the two adjacent sides which each appears to have two roofs; then the roof which they both share is the Window.

This can be confusing, initially, but it will get easier with practice. The "rule" for *intact* crystals (meaning no Imprints or partial points) is to count faces. Remember, if there are only six faces, no matter how convincing it is, you don't have a Window. Here's a cool hint: if you have a partial point, you can still determine a Window by looking for two adjacent sides (walls) which share a face (roof).

The next thing you do to further determine what kind of configuration you have is to count the *edges* of each face. This is easy if you start counting edges on the main face and again, work your way around the top of the crystal, counting the edges of each face. You are looking for faces with five edges (Isis), seven edges (Channelers, Transmitters or Dows) and eight edges (Eight-Sided Face or Grounding crystals).

You may have noticed the name Eight-Sided Face and wondered why it isn't called Eight-*Edged* Face. It is because edges of faces are also called sides. I know. I can hear what you're thinking; “Geeze, Genn! We have s*ides* of the crystal and *sides* of the face! Will I *ever* figure this out?!” Hang in there, you can do this! You will count the *edges* of the face, but then you will call them *sides*. For example; five-sided face, seven-sided face, eight-sided face, etc.

Let's get back to counting edges. Take each face as if it was a separate entity, and it will be easier. Beginning with the main face (remember, this is usually the largest one), put your thumb or finger on one of the edges of the face (to keep track of where you started). Discover the counting method that works best for you and use that one. Keep track of how many edges (sides) each face has.

It seems there are many things to check in order to figure out what crystal configuration you have. It is similar to unpeeling an onion. Looking under that skirt is far more complicated than you originally thought, isn't it? What's next?

After you have figured out which end is the termination and which is the base, how many faces you have, (whether you have any Windows) and then counted edges of each face, the next step is to look at surface features.

To view the surface (to keep from looking *inside* of the crystal), hold your crystal parallel to a light source so that you can use the glare that the light creates in order to see what is on the surface. Let me illustrate this for you.

Imagine a very clear lake. If the sun isn't shining off the surface, then you see right down into the lake and you can see rocks and fish and weeds, right? But when the glare of the sun is on the water, you can see things floating on the surface like dust, bugs, or even ripples that you wouldn't have been able to see without the sun's glare. The same is true for surface features on a crystal.

The best way to do this (and you will do it for each face) is to find your best light source, the sun if you are outside or a bright light or lamp if you are inside. Then, starting with the main face, work your way around the crystal by tipping it until you can see the surface features in the light's glare.

There may be etching, Record Keepers or scratches; sometimes, there are no markings at all. Other surface features you may find are covered more in-depth in the next chapter.

Moving from the surface features to the inside, crystals are rarely *completely* water clear. Usually they have something called Fairy Frost, which is caused from fractures and/or inclusions of air or moisture (teeny bubbles). As you might well imagine, when you combine a solution with movement and add heat and pressure, it is less likely to produce a crystal with pristine clarity. A crystal that is completely water clear through and through, with no fractures or inclusions, is called optically clear; this is rare. Usually crystals that are very water clear at the top will have some degree of Fairy Frost toward the base.

Crystals may have internal fractures caused by extreme temperature changes and/or movement during the growth process. We will discuss this more fully later, but it is also possible to fracture the inside of your crystal by "shocking" it from one temperature extreme to another; this is not recommended.

There are also crystals that have pockets of water in them. These are called Enhydro crystals and the only way you can tell if you have one is if the pocket of fluid also has an air bubble. I *love* Enhydro crystals! They emit an exciting bubbly energy when you turn them. The bubble will rise in the water channel…bloop bloop!

We talked about minerals that may be present in the solution when the crystal is forming. If the solution in which the crystal is forming is saturated with a mineral, that mineral may cover the growing crystal point. Remember the mud in the bathtub story? We're going to revisit crystal Phantoms.

As I said before, you may have only one, or there might be many layers of phantoms. Many layered phantoms which can be viewed through the side of a crystal occur when the solution in which a crystal is growing has a current or flow. Only one side of the phantom forms in these cases.

Layers of phantoms are created if the solution clears, is covered by another layer of clear crystal and mineral is reintroduced into the clear solution (creating phantoms) several times over.

To visualize what am I talking about when I speak of layered phantoms and single phantoms, imagine a little stacking Russian doll with the outermost doll being made of glass. Looking in, you only see the largest nested doll, right? There might be dolls inside dolls (phantoms inside phantoms), but you wouldn't see them unless you cut the bottom off the doll and looked in from the base.

In the case of a crystal, if there was more than one phantom and the bottom was polished, you would see the smallest phantom in the center and rings of phantoms out to the largest phantom. I have some crystals from Brazil like this.

Geologically, I'm sure there is much more to the *creation* of phantoms than I am describing here. However, because I am a crystal lover, not a geologist, I'm just describing the *presence* of phantoms in a way that is easy to visualize.

Broken, chipped and otherwise damaged crystals are called Empathic. Usually they are damaged in the mining process. Possibly they have been dropped and subsequently chipped, or dinged, by being dropped in the care of an individual. However the damage may occur, Empathic crystals bring out compassionate feelings in us.

What is the first thing you usually do when you see a chipped or damaged crystal? You say, "Oh... poor thing!" I tend to pet, pat, nuzzle or love a crystal that has been damaged; most people do. So the crystal picks up this empathy and amplifies it.

Who knows? A crystal being may actually *choose* to be damaged so that it will help us to be more compassionate!

As an example: I have a friend who found a small crystal point while digging crystal. He loved this crystal because it was "perfect". It had no chips or dings, and the termination was pristine. He wire wrapped it and wore it as a necklace.

Even though he was extremely careful, one day this crystal developed a small chip in the termination. It is my belief that the crystal chose to become chipped in order to help this friend to be more compassionate about the perfect imperfections within *himself.*

As we know, the lifetime of a crystal is much longer than ours. A chipped, damaged or dinged crystal will encounter many people during its lifespan, each of them feeling empathy for the damage on the crystal. It is a cycle that repeats. Even when an Empathic crystal finds its way to someone who may not understand or feel empathy for the crystal, the crystal continues transmitting empathetic feelings that will benefit the person who has somehow connected with that crystal.

In describing how to identify your crystal, there is a good amount of information to process. Let's review the usual progression I follow, step-by-step:

- Determine "top" from "bottom" and look for Lineation to determine sides.
- Find the main face to determine the "front."

- Check for any self-healing.
- Count the number of faces (any number over six means you have a Window).
- Count the number of edges to each face.
- Look at surface features.
- Check the inside for Fairy Frost, Phantoms, Manifestation points, etc.

Again, let me remind you there are no rules, and you don't have to follow this particular order. As with everything we have discussed, the best way to do this is the way it works for you.

Now that I have described the basic anatomy of a crystal point, let's take the time to talk specifically about the different configurations you might find in your crystals. A single crystal may have just one of these configurations or it may have many.

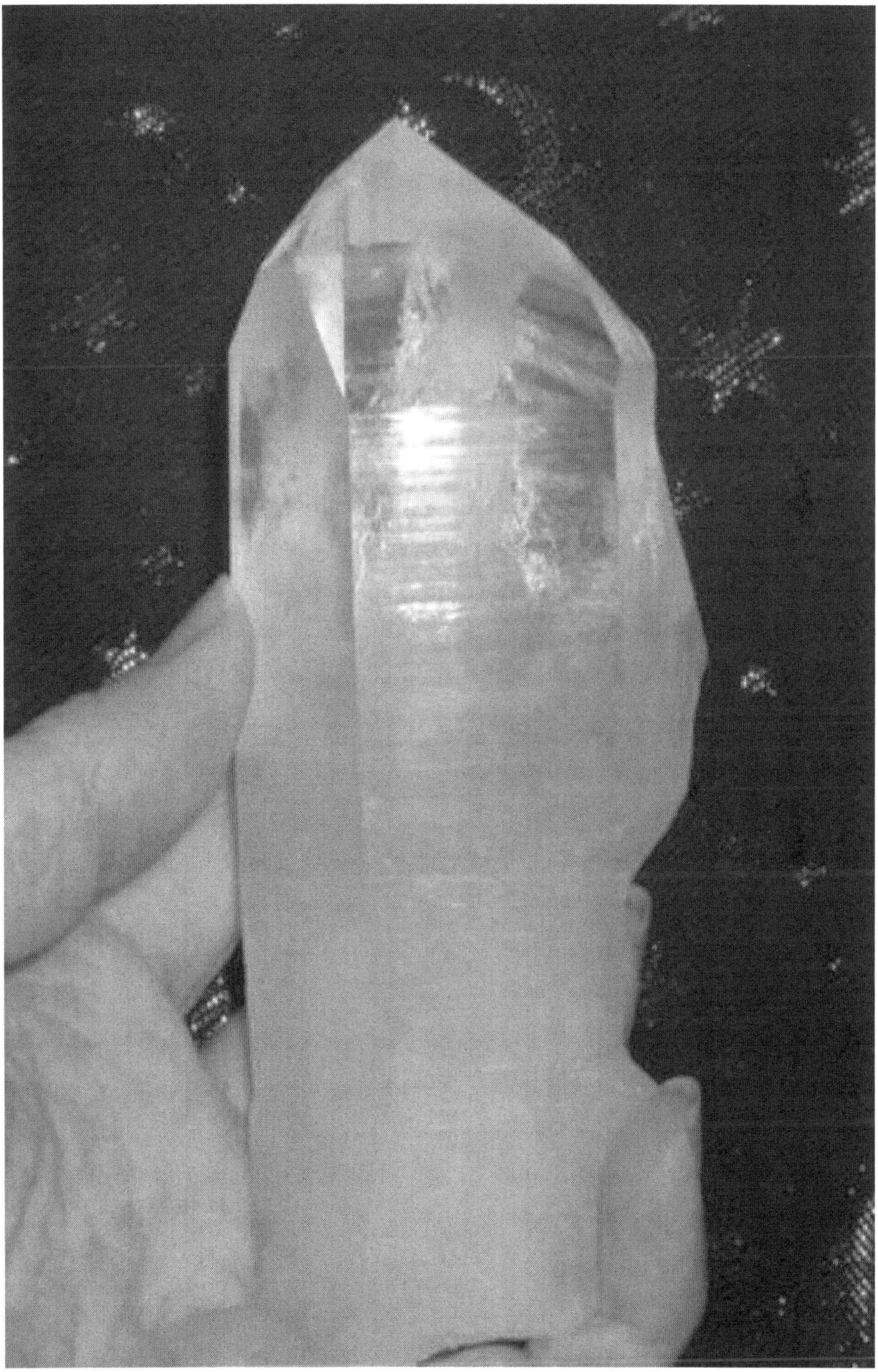

Configurations

Crystal configurations are varied and many.

Some of them have several different names, all describing the same thing. There are some that are quite common and others that are quite rare.

I'm not going to list every crystal configuration that has ever been named. Instead, I will list the most frequently occurring configurations that I have encountered (and yes, there are frequently occurring rare configurations, although that is a bit of an oxymoron, I know).

One reason to learn the names for these different configurations is so we're all on the same page when we are describing them to others. Naming the configurations also helps to provide us with a general guideline from which to begin if we need assistance in selecting a crystal for specific assistance.

I also don't believe that just because one person says this type of crystal is good for this one certain thing, that it is necessarily gospel. Your crystal may have come to you to help you with something entirely different than its structure may suggest.

Most crystal books include what seems like an endless list of properties for each type of crystal; so many, that when I first started learning, I couldn't hold even *one* of them foremost in my mind. For that reason, I have intentionally kept the properties lists brief.

I strongly encourage you to discover what each configuration means to you. I have left you space to record your *own* conclusions as you work with your crystal friends.

With each configuration, we will discuss the name (or names) most commonly used and then we will consider four areas:

- A drawing of the configuration;
- The physical description of how to identify it;
- The most common metaphysical characteristic; and

- A blank area for you to record your impressions as you work with that particular configuration.

Following is a note from Venus regarding configurations and a reminder of what she said in her introduction:

While a Record Keeper or another shaped configuration may be considered to serve a specific role which the current Lightworkers have agreed that they resonate better with, energies are expected to be found in these specific crystalline forms because the structure is such that certain vibrations transmit more freely within, so we choose to enhance and work through those energies and manifest in that way.

Regarding the different "types" of crystal, just as two humans are made of the exact same material, have the same organs, when sitting across from them, you are aware of their individuality. Even those whom you call twins, while they are exact in their makeup, down to even the cellular level, they are quite different. This is how it is with us as well.

So what I understand from Venus is this: energies may resonate within, and through, the different crystal shapes such as Generators, Tabbies, etc. However, just because a point may be a Generator or Tabby, it isn't necessarily going to emit the exact energy that another Generator or Tabby might.

Crystals are as individual and varied as people; you need to keep this in mind as you are working with your crystal friends.

Barnacle

Physical description: Barnacles are smaller crystals that are attached to a larger crystal. I have seen Barnacles called "babies" in some descriptions, but I see babies usually as one or two larger crystals standing at the feet of or attached to a crystal with a parental energy. There might just be a few Barnacles on a point, or they might encrust the point and look like jewels. Usually, these crystals emit a very Old Soul, ancient feeling.

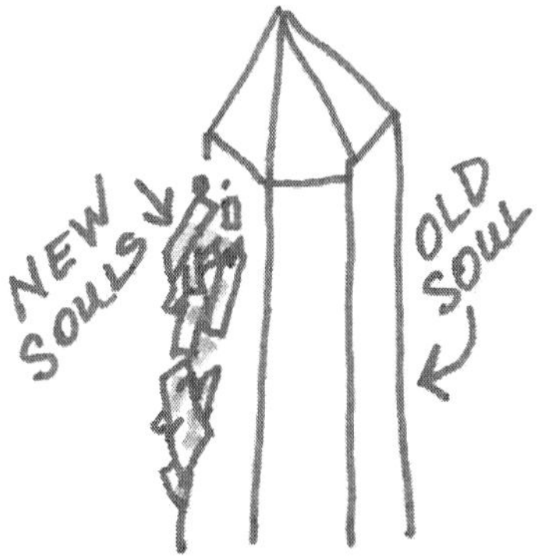

Metaphysical description: The larger crystal is the "Old Soul" and contains the wisdom and trust that attracts the smaller crystals (babies or new souls). I usually find that these Old Soul crystals with Barnacles are helpful to us in the way that a loving human grandmother/father or great grandmother/father would be (Imagine the Oracle from the Matrix movies). They help us to see things from a wider, deeper, wiser perspective. I think of the description of a crystal with Barnacles not so much as a description of the Barnacles themselves, but of the energy of the crystal that attracts or grows Barnacles.

NOTES

Bridge and/or Inner Child

Physical description: A Bridge or Inner Child is a smaller crystal (or crystals) penetrating and located partially in and partially out of a larger crystal. Both names, Bridge and Inner Child, are used interchangeably. I call them Bridges when the point is fairly large and the point seems to equally bridge inner to outer. The Inner Child crystals I see as much smaller and penetrating more "in" than "out" and they have a feeling to me of going "within." The drawings below are examples of how a smaller crystal may penetrate. A Bridge or Inner Child may be represented in either arrangement. Determining whether you have a Bridge of Inner Child depends on the size of the penetrating point and the energy presented.

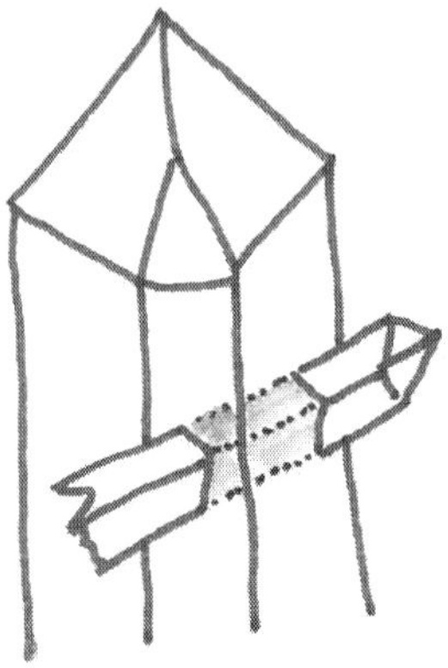

<u>Metaphysical description</u>: Bridge Crystals help to bridge between worlds. It may be the inner and outer worlds between your inner and outer Selves or between yourself and others in the physical environment in which you now live. They are helpful in any area you might imagine needing a bridge. They can help you heal and get in touch with your inner child (bridging the gap between your outer self and your inner self).

NOTES

___

___

___

___

___

___

___

___

___

Channeling or Channeler

Physical description: In order to determine if your crystal is a Channeler crystal, you must count the edges of the faces, as I described earlier. If it is a Channeler, the main face will have seven edges. Directly behind that seven-sided face, there will be a three-sided face (triangle). This configuration is described as a seven-three.

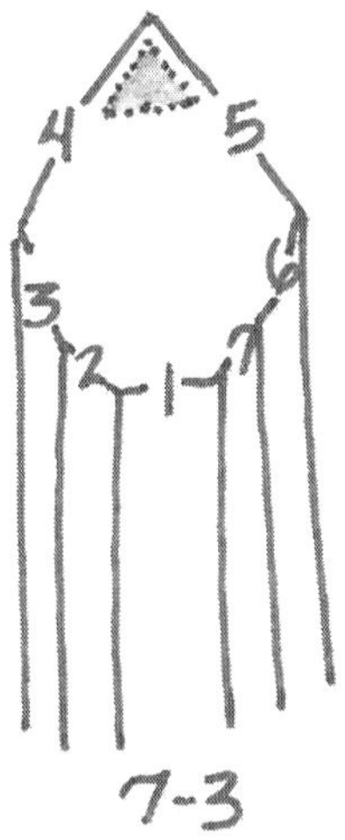

Metaphysical description: Channelers help you access higher wisdom, either in the form of your Higher Self or Spirit Guides, or of Angels. To me, these crystals exude a crisp, regal energy. Channeling crystals can bring you love and light from beings in the higher realms.

NOTES

Cluster

Physical description: Remembering the palms and fingers description, Clusters are points growing together on a matrix. Some Clusters grow on a sandstone matrix, others on all quartz, and still others may grow from a "seed" of crystal (such as a mass of double terminated points). Sometimes the Cluster will have a matrix that you can't see (in the same way that you can't see a porcupine's body when he is all curled into a ball, and yet you know he has one).

Metaphysical description: Clusters are good for helping with group dynamics. Families, co-workers, anywhere a group of people might need help in getting along. They are also good for raising the vibrations in an environment and bringing light and energy into that space.

NOTES

Curved

Physical description: Curved crystals have a curved shape or have sides that are curved. This happens when the crystal is forming and it is a rare occurrence. Sometimes just the sides are curved; sometimes the whole crystal looks bent. Sometimes they are self-healed into a curved or bent form.

Metaphysical description: Curved crystals have a gentle, yet powerful energy. They can be used to cleanse the aura. Very large ones can be used in a "scraping" fashion over the aura (you can actually feel the energy ripple after them). They help promote a flexible attitude.

NOTES

Double Terminated

Physical description: Double Terminated crystals have a termination on both ends. These crystals grow from a "seed" molecule of silicon dioxide in clay and grow outward in both directions. They are not formed on a matrix. The energy in these crystals flows in both directions as well. Even though they have two terminations, oftentimes there is usually one end that feels like the "top" and one that feels like the "bottom." Double Terminated points that are exactly the same on both ends don't have this top and bottom feeling, but they are rare. Double Terminated points can be single points or they may be clustered or grouped together.

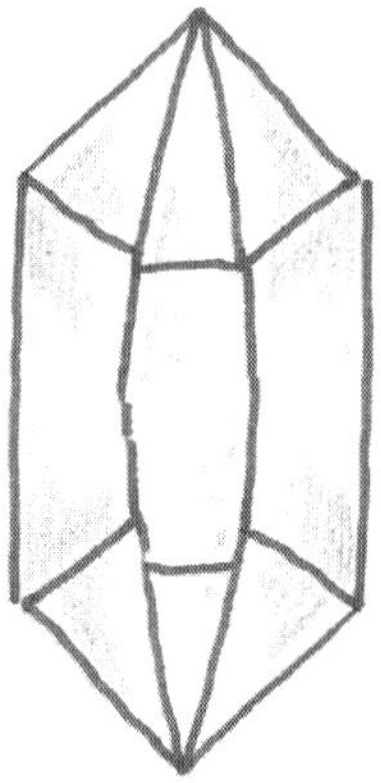

Metaphysical description: Double Terminated points promote psychic ability and dream recall (because they send as well as receive) and are also used for balance. They are useful in any application in which you want the energy to flow in both directions. I like using them in healing layouts or grids because the energy flows in both directions.

NOTES

Dow or Trans-Channeler

Physical description: This is an example of a crystal with two names for the same configuration. This configuration, called both Dow (named after Janeann Dow) as well as Trans-Channeler (because these crystals are both Channelers and Transmitters in configuration), is more commonly referred to as Dow. This is another crystal that you cannot correctly identify unless you count the edges of the faces. There will be three seven-sided faces with a triangular face between each of them. So sides of the six faces will look like seven-three-seven-three-seven-three. A text-book perfect Dow or Trans-Channeler will have symmetrically-sized faces and a centrally located tip. Others may be uneven in symmetry, but the count will be correct. These are still Dow crystals.

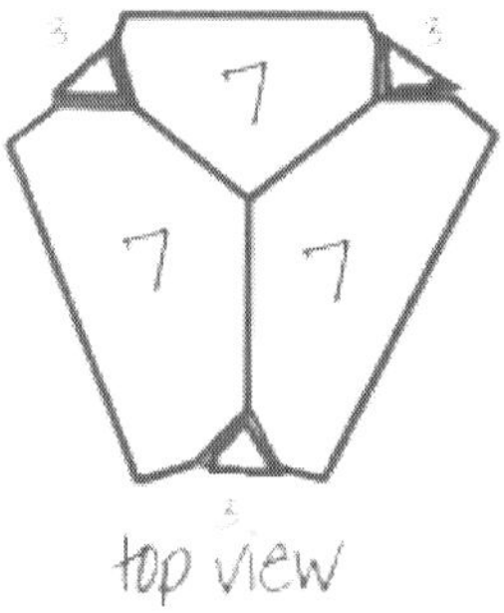

Metaphysical description: Dow or Trans-Channelers combine the qualities of the Transmitter and Channeler crystal. Dow crystals provide a connection with the self and Universal Truth. Dow crystals have a special energy about them that is sharp, clean and direct.

NOTES

Drusy (DREW-zee)

Physical description: Very similar to Barnacles, Drusy (sometimes spelled Druzy) consist of very small points that are described as "a myriad of very closely set tiny crystals." The Drusy clusters consist of tiny crystal points in their very formation, and are encrusted on either sandstone or quartz based matrixes. I like to call it "Sugar Drusy" because the tiny crystals making up the Drusy look like sugar crystals.

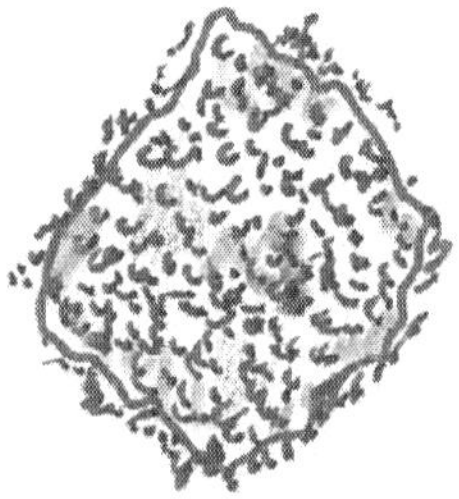

Metaphysical description: I think of Drusy crystals as assisting with ideas or thought forms ready to spring forth and grow. They have a soft, subtle and magical energy.

NOTES

Eight-Sided Face or Grounding Crystals

Physical description: These crystals are also called Grounding crystals, and they have eight edges on the main face. If you remember, I said generally each side or wall has a face or roof. While it isn't uncommon to have seven edges to a face, in the case of Eight-Sided Face crystals, there is an extra edge. This is a rare occurrence (there are still only six sides on the body of these crystals).

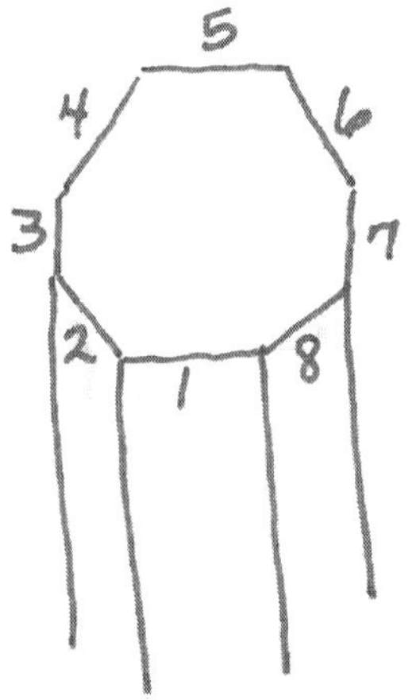

Metaphysical description: A stop sign also has eight sides; use this to remember that these crystals help you to stop and ground. I like to put my thumb on the grounding face (the largest face) and use it that way. You may also press and hold the grounding face to ground energy in any chakra.

NOTES

Elestial

Physical description: Elestial crystals have natural terminations over the body and face of an etched and/or layered crystal. What does that mean? They really aren't in the shape of a point. They are layered all over with self-healed looking surfaces. Sometimes points are what I call "Elestiated." To me that means it is a point that isn't quite all point, and isn't quite all Elestial, but sort of a combination of the two.

Metaphysical description: Elestial crystals have a soft, loving energy. They usually feel angelic to me. I use them when I want to connect to an angelic energy all around me. Their energy is less focused, more amorphous (having no definite form, without shape).

NOTES

Empathic

Physical description: Broken, chipped and otherwise damaged crystals are called Empathic. Usually they are damaged in the mining process. Even though they may survive the mining process without injury, sometimes they get dropped (for example in our homes) and subsequently are chipped or dinged.

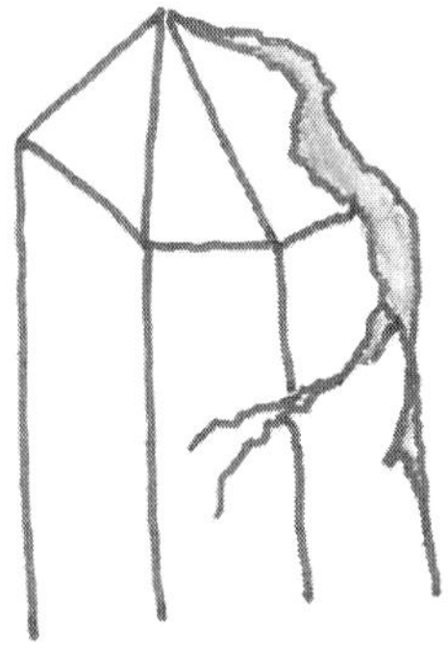

Metaphysical description: Empathic crystals bring out compassionate feelings in us. When we see a chipped or damaged crystal, we tend to show it love. The crystal picks up this empathy and amplifies it. An Empathic crystal will encounter many people during its lifespan and each person that expresses compassion for the damage on the point increases the empathetic energy of the point. It is a cycle that repeats. People who tend not to feel compassion still benefit from Empathic crystals because the crystals emit compassionate energy.

NOTES

Etched

Physical description: Etched crystals have abrasions on the outer areas of the crystal that look like hieroglyphics or writing of some sort. I've seen them called Lightning Strike Quartz, as well. I don't know exactly what causes the etching.

Metaphysical description: To me, the etching on crystals is symbolic in that it looks like writing. In the case of Lightning Strike, it looks like a lightning bolt zigzagging across. I feel that the best way to use these crystals depends on the particular shape the etching takes (refer to Sacred Sigil crystals). You frequently find Etching on Gas Phantoms.

NOTES

Extraterrestrial or ET

Physical description: Extraterrestrial crystals have a single termination at the top and the base has several large terminations. They remind me of a rocket ship. It is important to note the distinction between an ET crystal and a point with a cluster growing from the base. The extra terminations on ET crystals will not also have bodies attaching them to the main point whereas terminations on a cluster base would.

Metaphysical description: Extraterrestrial crystals have a powerful energy. You may use them to assist you in accessing beings from other realities (extraterrestrials) and Angels.

NOTES

Faden

FAH-den, from the German “faden” meaning thread.

Physical description: Faden quartz crystals have a fuzzy white thread-like area going side-to-side. I primarily find them in Tabby crystals, most especially Tabby clusters (two or more Tabby points attached side-to-side, as in the drawing below). The fuzzy “thread” reminds me of the white thing you sometimes find in chicken eggs when you scramble them (it is the umbilical cord of the embryo, I know, ugh). The energy in Faden crystals is sticky and connective like in the egg description but without the grossness factor.

Metaphysical description: Faden crystals are good for astral travel (silver cord) and connecting (thread). You may have a Faden crystal which spans just one crystal (or in the case of a Tabby cluster), between more than one crystal. Work with the Faden line in the crystal with that in mind. Faden lines in single crystals may help you connect within a certain realm or lifetime. If it spans between more than one crystal, you may travel between more than one realm, plane or even lifetime. You may also tap into the properties of both Tabby (communication) and Faden (connecting) to work with a connection between yourself and another.

NOTES

Fairy Frost

Physical description: Fairy Frost crystals have fractures and inclusions of air within them. The trapped air is wispy, white and fairy-looking. They are sometimes called Devic crystals. Lots of crystals have Fairy Frost. Some are more fairy-like than others.

Metaphysical description: Crystals with Fairy Frost are able to connect you with nature spirits and fairies (deva). They encourage us to connect with nature and to care for Mother Earth.

NOTES

Feminine

Physical description: Feminine crystals are dense and milky. The concentration of density in a Feminine crystal varies from nearly opaque fairy frost to solid white, milky quartz. Sometimes a crystal with some clarity (which typically is described as masculine) will still emit a feminine energy.

Metaphysical description: Feminine crystals help us (both men and women) to get in touch with our feminine nature. They have a soft, yet deep, mysterious energy. Yin in nature, Feminine crystals are intuitive, nurturing and receptive.

NOTES

Physical description: Generator crystals have six equally sized faces and a centrally located tip. It is very unusual to find such a precise configuration. You may find a point with the energetic qualities of a Generator, but the physical description may not be textbook perfect (the tip may be centrally located but all the faces may not be equally sized and each might not reach the tip). We discussed that crystals are commonly polished into Generator points. Remember the energy might not be as focused as a naturally occurring Generator because the internal structure is different.

<u>Metaphysical description</u>: Generator points are very good for focusing energy (as in crystal wands). All the energy is coming out the center of the point and is very powerful. They have a crisp, precise, very direct energy. Two good words to describe the energy of a Generator are focus and precision.

NOTES

Physical description: Initially, I was introduced to these beautiful crystals as Titanium Gas Phantoms. There is a lot of controversy as to what creates them and if titanium is even involved. I choose to call them simply Gas Phantoms. The mine where they were found in Arkansas is now closed, and, as far as I know, they don't plan to re-open it. The faces of Gas Phantoms have a sort of gaseous-looking spray that looks like spreading fingers from bottom to top (base of triangle to tip). The really good examples have the spray marking as well as alternating clarity on every other face: one with a light, blue-grey haze (sometimes with a spray), the next clear, one with haze, one clear, etc. They usually have heavy etching on the faces, but not always. The spray looks like a bluish-grey to white haze or smoke just under the surface and the sides tend to have this smoky haze as well.

Metaphysical description: Gas Phantoms are excellent crystals for Lightworkers and those working with the emerging earth energies. I can't say enough how much I love these points! While they feel very powerful, their energy is buttery smooth and they have a soft feel.

NOTES

Golden Healer

Physical description: Golden Healers are quartz crystals that are partially or totally covered with a transparent golden-yellow mineral which has a thin coating of clear crystal. The coating ranges from iridescent yellow to darker orange, from total coverage to skippy, partial coverage. They may have rainbow iridescence called Natural Rainbow Aura on the outer layer (like rainbows you see on oil slicks). These points emit an especially high energy.

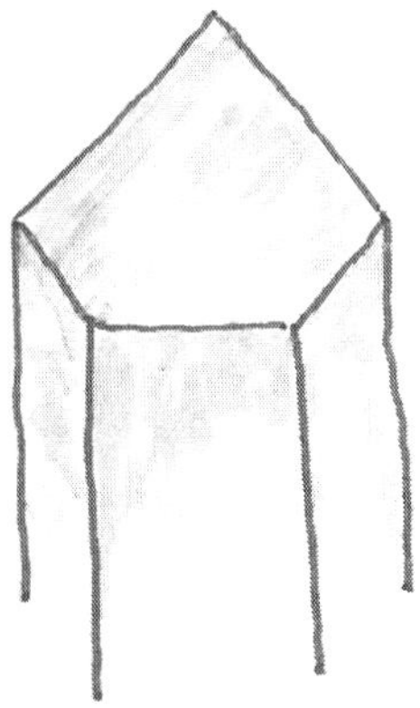

Metaphysical description: Golden Healer crystals are good for healing. They have a soft, bright energy. The lightly coated Healers have an enthusiastic and helpful liveliness in their aura. You don't even have to pick them up to experience this shift. The Golden Healers with a thicker, denser coating have a more serious energy. Golden Healers are one good example of very small points having as much energy as a very large point, ounce for ounce (the ant versus human comparison).

NOTES

Growth Interference

Physical description: Growth Interference crystals have missing areas in the main point where another mineral was growing during the development of the crystal and then subsequently disappeared. Lots of times it looks like a buzz saw was taken to the crystal. There used to be a mineral present that isn't there anymore, so they sort of look magical to me. Sometimes there is a little bit of mineral left in part of the crevasse.

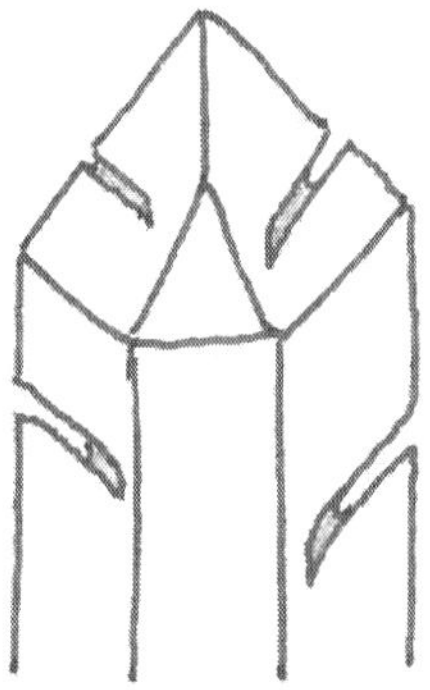

Metaphysical description: The properties of Growth Interference crystals are a bit like crystal Imprints. They represent how we can adapt and grow around a certain situation (or person), and then if the situation no longer serves, it leaves, but not without leaving a mark.

NOTES

Imprint

Physical description: Imprints are indentations or marks left on the sides or faces of a crystal where they grew in close proximity to another crystal. I haven't found reference to these marks in any crystal book. I suppose, technically, that they might fall into the "key" category.

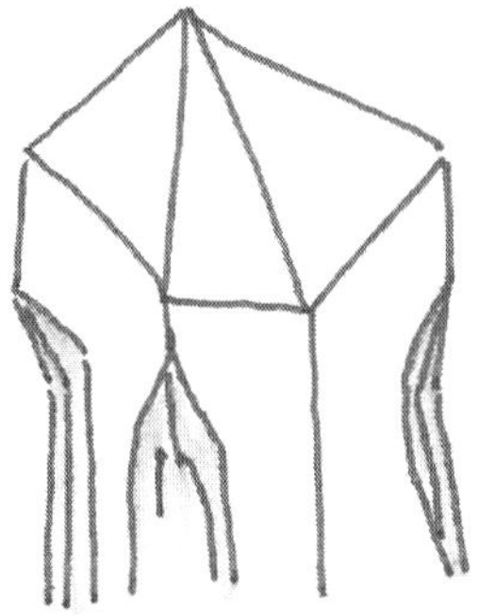

Metaphysical description: Crystals with Imprints show how something is affected by outside influences. The original structure adapts to its environment as outside influences change its shape or form. This allows for growth and change, while still maintaining its basic inherent truth and beauty.

NOTES

Inclusions

Physical description: When crystal is forming, there may be other substances present in the solution. These substances might be air bubbles or other minerals. They become trapped within the crystal point during its growth and are called Inclusions. Air and moisture inclusions fall into the category of Fairy Frost, a non-mineral inclusion.

Metaphysical description: The properties of these crystals will vary, depending on the mineral included within the crystal. The properties of the included mineral will be enhanced and amplified by being trapped within the structure of quartz.

NOTES

Isis Face

Physical description: An Isis Face is a five-sided face on a crystal point. To "qualify" as an Isis face, the edges are usually symmetrical like the one pictured. While the Isis Face in the illustration below is the main (largest) face, they are not always the largest face on the termination.

Metaphysical description: Isis Face crystals have a distinct feminine energy (even if the point appears very clear and masculine). An Isis Face point usually feels majestic and feminine (much as you would expect a goddess such as Isis to feel.) Isis Face crystals help you connect to all Goddess energy, not just the goddess Isis.

NOTES

Key

Physical description: A Key on a crystal point is an indentation left by the body of another crystal (either the tip base). Technically a key is really more like a key hole. It is a three or six- sided indentation in the side or face of a point. Sometimes you will see just a partial key where only part of the key is present (like the key on the right side in the illustration). Other times you may find a six-sided indentation encircling the base of a point, and in these cases, I suppose that point is the one which caused a Key in another crystal.

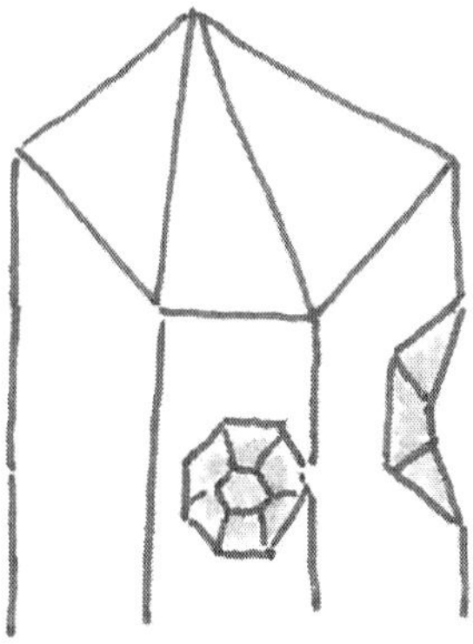

Metaphysical description: Key crystals are good to help you unlock answers to questions you may have. Keys open doors.

NOTES

Laser Wand

Physical description: Laser Wand crystals are thicker at the base than the tip. The termination is usually quite small in comparison to the rest of the point. While the body of the point may not be curved, the edges of the sides are often curved and heavily lineated. Lemurian Seed Crystals are usually (but not always) in the shape of a Laser Wand.

Metaphysical description: Laser Wands are good in both inner and outer work. I find them to have a very precise, narrow focus. Imagine writing with a mechanical pencil versus a crayon.

NOTES

Lightbrary or Cathedral

Physical description: These crystals are comprised of a main point surrounded by smaller points, some of which merge into the main point. If you can imagine a sand castle, that's what these crystals look like. The surrounding points may not be whole (as in crystals attached side-by-side), but instead are actually merged into the main crystal. I haven't seen a lot of these Lightbraries (with the points surrounding the main crystal); they are rare. I have seen more of them that are partial (a main point with two or three merged points surrounding it). There are merged points that are not necessarily Lightbraries. There is a different energy to the main or central crystal of Lightbraries.

Metaphysical description: Lightbraries are extremely powerful Lightworkers and are full of wisdom. They transmit very high vibration and can be used to raise your vibrational frequency. The smaller points contain information from the Akashic records.

NOTES

Lineated Sides or Lineated Face

Physical description: Lineated Sides are horizontal striations across the sides of a point; these are the crystals we talked about unzipping with your thumb. Points may also be Lineated on the faces. These surface markings are viewed in the same way you find Record Keepers. Lineation on a face starts as a small triangle that is outlined continually until the pattern runs off the face of the crystal. To picture this, just imagine the lines in a Zen garden. The innermost triangle may or may not be centrally located.

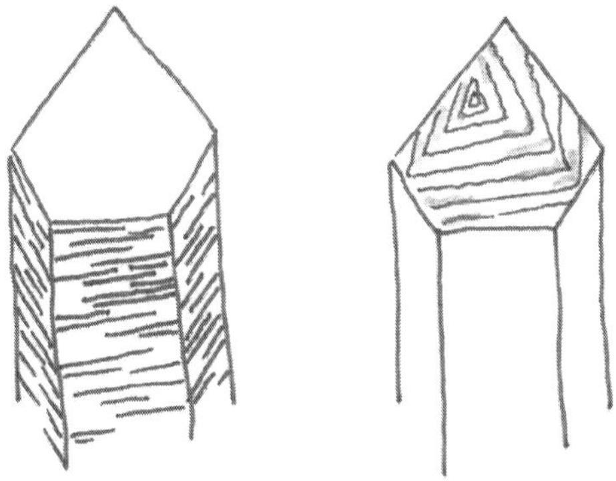

Metaphysical description: Deeply Lineated Sides may be unzipped to access further knowledge within the crystal. I experience this as receiving a deeper knowing or understanding that seems to be released quietly after they are unzipped. Lineated Faces may be accessed during meditation in the same way that you might use a labyrinth. To work with them, follow the lines in and down to a meditative state and when you are finished, work your way back out from the center.

NOTES

Physical description: Manifestation points are small points that have formed within a larger point; these are quite rare. They have a special energy to them that is difficult to describe. It is almost like a pregnancy, or a feeling of expectation inside. There is fullness in the energy a Manifestation point exudes. The Manifestation point refers to both the point within the main crystal as well as the main crystal itself. I can usually feel a Manifestation point by its special energy before I actually see it within the main crystal.

Metaphysical description: Manifestation points are powerful manifestors, which should come as no surprise. They may assist in the manifesting of many things, but for the best results, it is wise to focus on a single desire.

NOTES

Masculine

Physical description: Very clear points are Masculine. They may be optically clear, or they may have some Fairy Frost. The base of a Masculine crystal may be dense with frost, however if more of the point is clear than cloudy, it is described as Masculine. Remember not to have pre-conceived notions. Just because a point is masculine by description doesn't automatically mean it can only present masculine energy (the same is also true for Feminine crystals).

Metaphysical description: Masculine points are helpful when you need to get to the point; they have a sharp and direct energy. Yang in nature, Masculine crystals are more action-oriented and the energy projects rather than recedes.

NOTES

Phantom

Physical description: Phantoms exist within a main crystal when a mineral present in the solution has drifted down onto a crystal point during its growth. The mineral is subsequently grown over (trapped inside) with more clear crystal forming around it. Phantoms may be partial or complete. A Phantom will exactly mirror the actual terminating point of a crystal; if it doesn't, then you can be sure the termination has been polished or altered.

Metaphysical description: Phantoms are good for past-life work. The metaphysical properties of the minerals present are enhanced or amplified by the quartz. The properties will vary depending on what the mineral is (for example chlorite, hematite, etc.).

NOTES

Rainbow

Physical description: Rainbows may be present inside a crystal due to fractures or on the internal wall of two connected crystals. Some of the fractures are what I call mirror fractures; they look like mirrors and sometimes are called Wall crystals. Rainbows may be just pink and green, or they may have the full rainbow color spectrum. They often occur on the inner "wall" where two crystals have grown together. It is helpful to have very bright light, and you may have to turn the crystal (side-to-side, upside down, etc.) in order to see them. The rainbows aren't always in an arc shape unless the surface on which they occur is curved.

Metaphysical description: Rainbows are a gift from the Spirit Keeper in the crystal. Rainbow crystals are optimistic and happy. They remind us that we are loved.

NOTES

Record Keeper or Recorder

Physical description: Record Keepers (also called Recorders) are crystals that have triangular markings on the faces. They seem to be three-dimensional, but they usually can't be felt with your finger. You have to hold a crystal at just the right angle in order to see the Record Keeper. Usually they are very sharply edged, equilateral triangles; however, I have seen them with rounded bottoms as well (more arrowhead or even teardrop shaped). There may only be one present on a face, or you may find layers and layers of them. Record Keepers will appear and disappear (I call that "popping"). It is said that a Record Keeper crystal will find its way to the person who needs the information it contains.

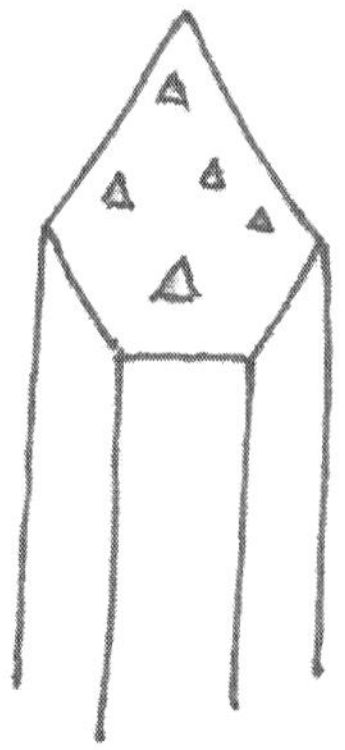

Metaphysical description: Record Keepers contain special wisdom. I don't know how that works exactly, but I also don't know how a CD can hold a sentence much less a whole encyclopedia. Suffice it to say that they represent storage devices and that the information was placed there by someone, perhaps in Atlantis or Lemuria. I love Record Keepers, they have a special energy.

NOTES

Self-Healed

Physical description: Self-Healed crystals are crystals that have been broken from the matrix and started to re-seal their broken end with new growth. A Self-Healed crystal looks like it has scales or triangular layers. Self healing can be present on the bottom, sides or even tip of a point or cluster. Self-Healed points also present as crystals that were broken in half but sort of "glued" back together with new growth.

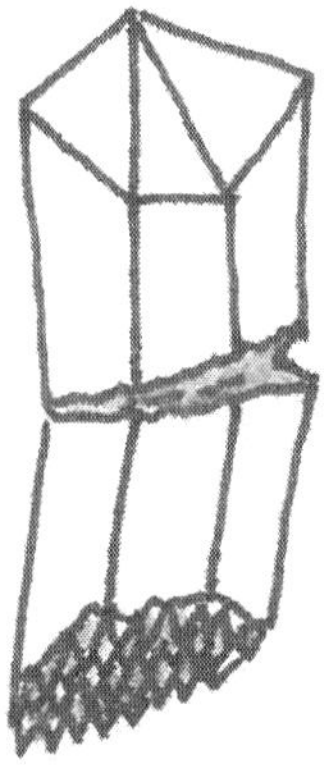

Metaphysical description: Self-healed crystals are good for healing, and they have sturdy, optimistic persistent energy. They are not quitters!

NOTES

Sacred Sigils

Physical description: Sacred Sigils are any markings that represent an idea. For example, a dollar sign is a sigil that represents money and abundance. Crystals may have markings that resemble things such as snake skin, mountain ranges, water or even cities. I have seen many crystals that have three-dimensional cities made of layers of buildings that look like pueblos on the surface. Sigils are surface features; you view them the same way you view a Record Keeper.

Metaphysical description: Because a Sacred Sigil is a marking that reminds us of an idea or invokes a memory or feeling, the meaning will depend on what shape the sigil is in and what that particular sigil represents to you.

NOTES

Physical description: A Sheet crystal is a very thin, flat piece of crystal, thinner than a Tabby and often self-healed. Usually, Sheet crystals don't have six sides to them, and they aren't always self-healed on all sides. Often, the broad, flat, sides are either lineated or self-healed. If there is an area that isn't self-healed, it will be on the thin edge. If at least one of the broad flat sides is not either a side (which you can determine if it has Lineation) or self-healed, it doesn't qualify as a Sheet crystal.

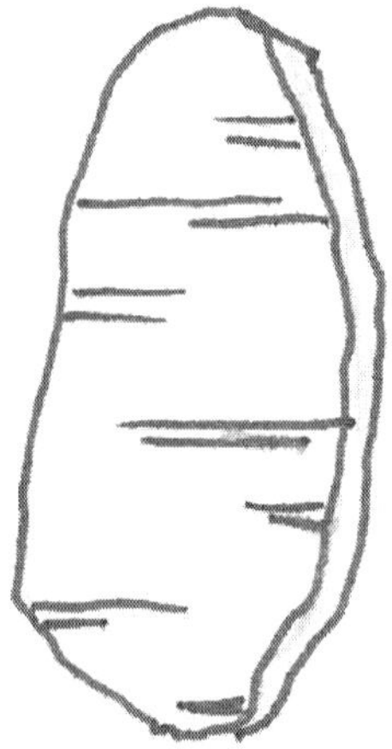

Metaphysical description: Sheet crystal is good for scrying and it has an expansive energy. They also often have a ringing bell-like sound when touched together.

NOTES

Smoky

Physical description: Smoky crystals are caused when a crystal is exposed to radiation. They may be natural or irradiated by man. Typically, natural Smoky crystals are usually a lighter grey/brown than crystals which have been artificially irradiated; these are usually almost black. It is possible to find very dark (almost black) natural Smoky quartz but usually it tends to be lighter in color. The only way to know for certain whether a point is naturally or artificially radiated is to ask the person where the point originated.

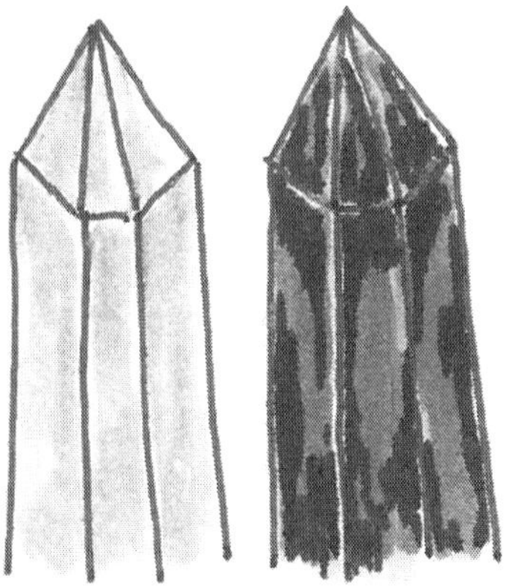

<u>Metaphysical description</u>: Smoky crystal is a good grounding stone. It is also elevating to your mood because it grounds and picks up your negativity. If you use it for this purpose, be sure to cleanse your Smoky quartz frequently.

NOTES

Soul Mate or Twin Soul

Physical description: The crystal names Soul Mate and Twin Soul can be used interchangeably. They are two crystals of a similar size grown side-by-side. Some faces of the crystals are exactly parallel to each other. This means they are on the same growth plane. You can tell this by holding them parallel to a light source the same way you view surface features on a point. You will be able to see if each face is on the same growth plane because they will both shine with the same glare. Sometimes the two points are simply side by side, and not aligned on the same growth plane. However a Soul Mate is a Soul Mate. I just wanted you to know more about the different ways they may present.

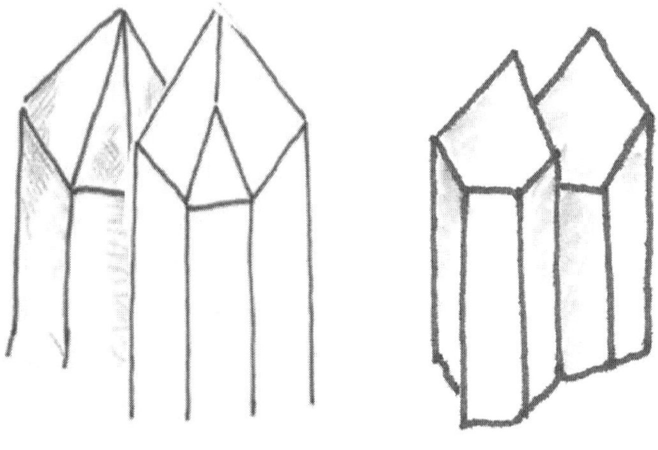

Metaphysical description: Soul Mate or Twin Soul crystals are able to assist us in our search for a mate; just don't expect to be able to put one by your chair at night and expect it to zap Prince or Princess Charming to your side by morning. This crystal can definitely assist you in attaining an appropriate energy for attracting a mate. They are also helpful in relationships, to promote loving contact and togetherness.

NOTES

Tabular or Tabby

Physical description: Tabular or Tabby crystals are thin, flat crystals. To "qualify" as a Tabby, they should be no more than half as thin as they are wide. For example, if a crystal is one inch wide it needs to be one-half inch thick or less in order to be called a Tabby. If it is two inches wide it needs to be one inch thick or less, etc.

Metaphysical description: Tabby crystals are good helpers with communication. I remember this because they are shaped like a tablet. Large Tabby crystals are also wonderful in healing applications due to their wide, flat shape.

NOTES

Physical description: Basically, a Transmitter is two Channeling faces side by side with a triangle in between (seven-three-seven). The main "face" or front is actually the "three" between the two seven-sided faces. The two seven-sided faces will be close to the same size. Sometimes one of the two faces is much larger than the other. I call these Transmitter crystals with a Channeler orientation.

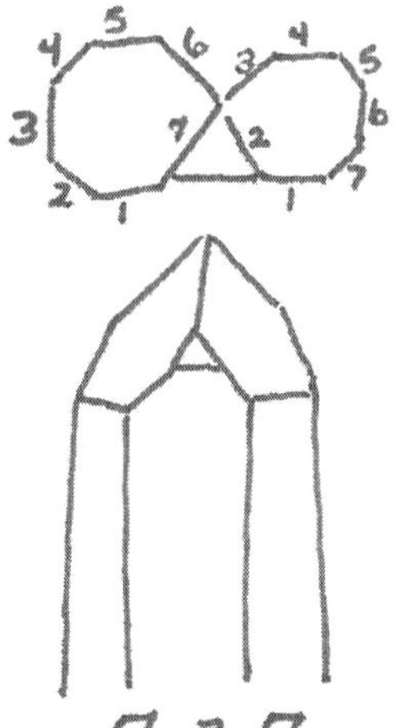

7-3-7

Metaphysical description: Transmitters work much like Channelers, only double! They help you access higher wisdom, either in the form of your Higher Self or Spirit Guides, or even Angels. Transmitters have a proud, almost mysterious, feel. I picture them as two sentinels standing not quite side-to-side and not quite back-to-back. I like them because their main face is between two diagonals. What do I mean by this? Imagine standing in front of a triangularly shaped building that has its entrance on the corner where the two sidewalks meet. It is unexpected and special.

NOTES

Trigonic Record Keeper

Physical description: A Trigonic Record Keeper is an upside-down Record Keeper that you can easily feel and see. They are like tiny Keys, actually, except that they are shaped like a Record Keeper (triangle) and the flat "bottom" of the triangle is at the top, the point is facing down. These may be present on the faces or sides of a crystal. They are rare.

Metaphysical description: These are crystals of transition. They are good for soul retrieval and can work as a key to the future. They have an interesting and unique energy. I think they feel like a traditional Record Keeper on steroids. The energy of a traditional Record Keepers is one of a quiet exciting knowledge or information held within the crystal itself. Trigonic Record Keepers feel more like a doorway to endless information. The energy of a traditional Record Keeper is likened to opening a book, whereas accessing the knowledge of a Trigonic Record Keeper is comparable to walking into a library.

NOTES

Window Crystal

Physical description: A Window crystal is a crystal with an extra diamond-shaped facet. Ideally, the diamond-shaped window face is large, but this is not always the case. Remember how I described determining if the face is one of the six regular faces or if it is a Window? If you have more than six faces, you need to determine which one is the Window. To do this, start at the top end of the side (bottom of the face) and work your way up to the tip. Generally any face that reaches toward the tip and has a side for its bottom is one of the six faces. If it seems to be trapped between a face and a side, it is a Window. You will find exceptions to this, especially on some of the more difficult crystals to read. It may take some practice to master this skill. It is possible for a crystal to have a Window (diamond shape) and also a Left Activation and Right Activation Window all in the same point!

Metaphysical description: Window crystals are good for scrying and accessing other realms, as well as accessing our own soul (window to the soul).

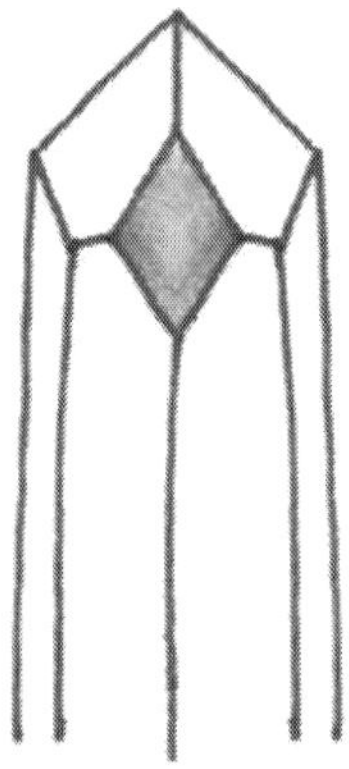

NOTES

Left Activation Window

Physical description: A Left Activation Window is an extra facet that leans to the left. It looks like a parallelogram leaning left. They may be sliver-thin or thick. It may remind you of a back slash on a computer keyboard.

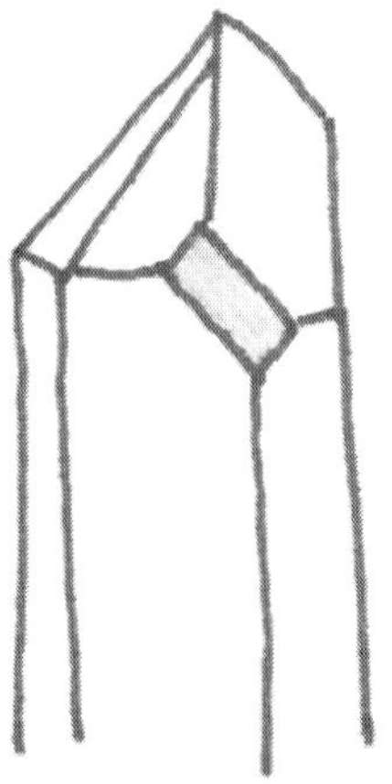

Metaphysical description: These are time links to the past. They also activate left-brain functions (such as logical thinking and analysis). If you are inclined to be more in one "brain" or the other, it is good to use the crystal of the hemisphere you tend not to use as much. Once you have reached a balance, you should work with a Left and a Right Activation crystal together to maintain that balance.

NOTES

Right Activation Window

Physical description: A Right Activation Window is an extra facet that leans to the right. It looks like a parallelogram leaning right. They also may be sliver-thin or thick. It may remind you of a forward slash on a computer keyboard.

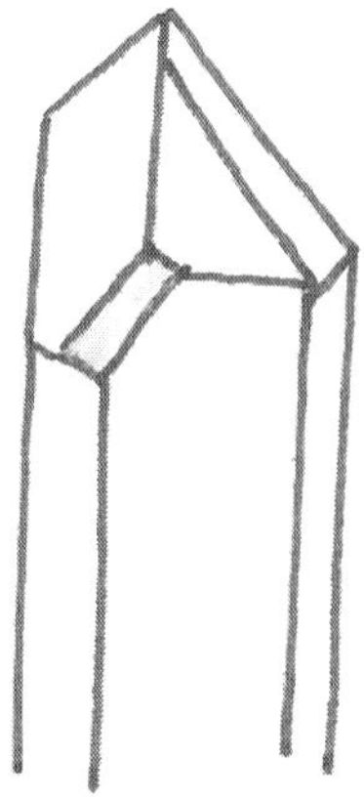

Metaphysical description: These are time links to the future. They also activate right brain functions (such as creativity, imagination and daydreaming). Just as with the Left-Activation Crystal, work with the crystal of the hemisphere you tend to use less, and once you attain balance, work with both together.

NOTES

Yin/Yang

Physical description: Yin/Yang crystals are half feminine and half masculine. They present as half cloudy and half clear. The base of a Yin/Yang point may be completely milky or just very densely clouded with Fairy Frost (almost white) and the top part may be clear with a little wispy Fairy Frost.

Metaphysical description: Knowing that Yin/Yang crystals have an equal measure of masculine to feminine energy, they are good for attaining and maintaining balance.

NOTES

Cleansing and Charging

Compact discs, computer memory, even cassette tapes all hold information. How they do it, I haven't a clue. It's like an invisible technological puzzle to me. Even if we do not know how they work, we can all agree that they do, indeed, hold memory. You can either buy them pre-programmed, or you can record your own.

What I'm attempting to do with these file and memory comparisons is to better help you understand crystals and how they function regarding programming and memory.

Crystals compare to humans, yes, but they also compare to computers. They store memories, senses, feelings and factual information, just like we do. However they are more like computers in that they are able to hold information for an indefinite period of time; so, too, is the information more accurate than when compared to the subjectivity of humans.

We're going to begin this section by talking about CLEANSING your crystal.

Erasing prior energy signatures is basically what it means to cleanse a crystal.

If you buy a crystal from a store, find one on the ground, or are gifted one from a friend, it is wise to cleanse it. Crystal easily picks up and amplifies energy, and because you don't know who or what they have come into contact with, it is a good idea to cleanse any new crystals.

It is like an energetic bath, so to speak.

Sometimes the crystal will feel “full” or “sticky” energetically, so you will need to cleanse your crystal friend of the excess absorbed energies.

When would you need to cleanse a crystal?

- When it first arrives in your home;
- After using it for healing or intense energy work;
- After a particularly negative experience.

It is wise to cleanse your crystal once a month, even if you aren't actively working with your crystal because you can be assured *it* is working with *you*.

Cleansing your crystal begins with intent and while there are many different ways to do this, the one thing they all have in common is intent.

What is important is *intent*, not *content*.

If you decide that the best way for you to cleanse your crystal is to stand on one foot, shut one eye, cross your toes and recite the ABC's backwards, then by all means do it! I am just going to give you some basic suggestions for cleansing, all of which are much easier to do than the ABC toe-crossing example.

You may choose to cleanse them wet or dry, with smoke (by smudging) or herbs. Just please remember this mantra throughout: "*Intent not Content*". What you intend to do will always override what you actually do.

In essence, this means that *you really can't make a mistake if your intent is pure.*

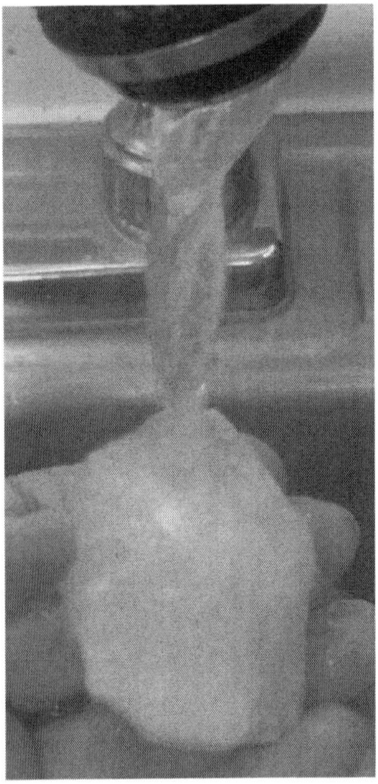

Water is a great way to cleanse your crystal, so that it becomes receptive and energetically "clean."

CAUTION: if you choose this method, be certain that you match the temperature of the crystal to the temperature of the water.

For example, if your crystal is cold, use cold water. If it is warm, use warm water.

The best way to do this is to hold your crystal in one hand and run the water over the other and adjust the heat until the temperatures are roughly equal. I don't mean to the exact degree; this isn't rocket science.

However, if you "shock" your crystal by placing it in a temperature very different from itself, you can shatter the inside or even break it (for instance dropping a cold crystal into a hot bath or a hot crystal into a cold bath). I am told that they don't like it physically and they also don't like it energetically. It is jarring, but more importantly it *indicates to them that you aren't being mindful while you are cleansing.* Testing the temperature causes you to be connected with your crystal and fully present in the now.

Once you have the temperature adjusted, hold your crystal under the running water and while visualizing the cleansing, thank it for the work it has been doing on the behalf of humanity.

As a consideration, there are some stones that will dissolve in water. Obviously you shouldn't use water as a cleansing method for these minerals. Use caution with minerals other than quartz; check online or refer to information concerning your specific crystal.

The question of whether or not to use salt water for cleansing always comes up, to which my answer is most always no. (Seawater is a different case.)

If you have used this method in the past, don't worry that you have been torturing your crystals or intentionally harming them in some way. If you find that your particular crystal is not opposed to salt water, use your intuition. Remember there are no hard and fast rules. I've been told by the Crystal People that salt water can be much too harsh; it has to do with the ions of sodium chloride in the solution.

If you prefer to use salt for cleansing, consider using it dry. A bed of sea salt with some lavender, sage, or another favorite dry herb mixed in might be quite nice. You may want to place a natural cloth (such as cotton or silk) over the salt and then nestle the crystal down onto the cloth for an overnight cleanse rather than burying them directly in the salt.

Herbs are another nice option to use for cleansing your crystal. Lavender, sage, sweet grass; whatever herb you prefer. You may choose to nestle your crystal into a bed of the dry herbs. You may also use the smoke from herbs as a cleansing tool.

Burning incense or sage is great. Light your herb (sage, sweet grass, incense, etc.) and run the crystal back and forth in the smoke.

Whichever method you choose; water, dry salt, herbs or smoke, what are you also doing? You're *intending* that the method of choice is cleansing the crystal of prior energetic signatures.

Sometimes crystals we newly adopt have been in the house of a smoker or an infrequent duster. The best way to *physically* cleanse your crystal is water and a mild soap. Don't forget to be mindful of matching the temperature. Use mild dish soap with a toothbrush and scrub-a-dub-dub. Crystals like it when you sing to them while you scrub behind their ears.

Running water in a stream can be used to energetically cleanse your crystal, as well, but consider putting your crystal in the toe end of a knee-high pantyhose or sock if you're going to leave it in the stream.

A very good friend of mine put all his healing stones in a stream (in a colander or something similar) and when he went back the next morning he realized a storm upstream had markedly increased the water flow where his crystals were bathing; he nearly lost them all. Luckily, he had a dam of sorts and they didn't go too far. A nylon or knee-high sock works well for preventing this kind of mishap. Don't forget to anchor it to the bank.

If you decide to use a stream for cleansing, remember the above warning about temperature. Obviously, you can't change the temperature of the stream. If it is a cold stream, just be sure you haven't had your crystal out sunbathing on a rock prior to taking it for a swim; because crystal doesn't pick up heat like other rocks it *will* feel cooler than the surrounding stones, however great temperature discrepancies are still dangerous to your crystal. I simply recommend using common sense.

Crystals can be bathed in moonlight or sunlight to cleanse them as well. Sunlight is fine for clear (meaning non-colored) crystals, but if you have colored crystals (such as Amethyst, Citrine, Rose Quartz, etc.) sunlight (even inside on a windowsill) can fade your colored crystal to clear, so use extreme caution.

For cleansing crystals which you have programmed for a specific task, a growing (waxing) moon (new moon going to full) is good for crystals which you work with on things that you want to increase (abundance, love, concentration, success, etc).

The energy of a diminishing (waning) moon (from full moon to new) is good for cleansing crystals that help you with things that you want to decrease (excess weight, anger, procrastination, fear, etc).

Choose the appropriate moon and set your crystals out for some great cleansing and energetic bathing.

Crystals should be cleansed when you get them, but they should also be cleansed periodically as you work with them. Watching the moon phase helps you to remember to cleanse and charge your working crystal at least monthly. We'll discuss charging in more detail later.

What if you live in a cave in which the sun or moonlight never penetrates, you don't get satellite reception, your cell phone doesn't work, and you don't have access to herbs or water? Man I would hate to be you right about now! We've described all the "what if you don't have's." You *do* have your crystal friend and you *do* have your intent. That's all you need.

Next time you and your crystal friend are locked up in the gulag and you worry about how you are going to cleanse or clear, all you need is your *positive attitude* and your *intent.* You can accomplish anything you want with those two ingredients.

If you have so many crystals you can't possibly move them all to be cleansed, simply respectfully *think* them cleansed, and it is done. If you prefer a ritual, visualize whatever you need to visualize, burn sage and blow it around the room, light incense, and request that your crystal friends receive the cleansing that they need.

Likewise, if you have a reason you can't safely burn incense or sage; wave an unlit bundle of sage around. Skip and hop with one eye shut and talk like a pirate "Aye! Me crystals all be cleansed as this sage bundle be waved to and fro! ARR!" (One of my favorite Spirit Guides is a sea-going man… that's for you, Skully! Arr!)

Or simply intend them to be cleansed by the energies of the moon; they will hear you and receive your intention. The important thing is that you don't simply plop them down into a room and forget about them entirely.

You may also cleanse your crystals in a way that doesn't involve any physical action from you. There are stones such as Selenite that don't require cleansing; you can keep Selenite with your crystals and it will cleanse them for you. You still don't want to forget all about them, though.

The key concept in all endeavors which have to do with our crystal friends is that we maintain a connection with them in whatever way works best for us, as long as we keep the connection.

Let's move on from *cleansing* and discuss *charging.*

CHARGING is similar to refilling the crystals' "battery."

Compare it to giving it a vacation from work to rest and rejuvenate.

Charging is as individualized as cleansing. There is no "one right way." In my opinion there is no "one right way" for anything.

The description of *how* to charge your crystal is nearly identical to the moonlight cleansing technique we mentioned earlier, so the description on how to charge your crystal will seem much shorter. In the moonlight, cleansing and charging can happen simultaneously. The difference is that *cleansing* is an energetic bath (a *releasing* of energies) whereas *charging* is an energetic upload (a *gathering* of energies).

Crystals benefit from the energies of the moon by becoming charged with the lunar energy. We discussed using the waning moon for *cleansing* crystals which are helping with decreases. For *charging* these crystals, however, (remember, charging is *gathering* energies), full moon energy is preferred because at this time the lunar energies are at their greatest.

If it's not feasible to move your crystals into the direct moonlight they are still benefitting from the lunar influence. The moon energies can, and do, reach and affect us, even if we aren't right under the moonbeams.

If you prefer the energies of the sun, apply the lunar charging techniques and substitute “sun” for “moon” being sure to remember the caution about colored crystals and fading.

Okay, our crystals are cleansed and charged, so what do we do now?

Clearing and programming are up next!

Recording what you want assistance with is the basic premise behind programming a crystal.

You simply determine what kind of assistance you would like from your crystal friend, and then respectfully ask the crystal to help you. I talked about saving files to a computer earlier; it's basically the same thing.

With *focused intent* and a *clear request*, it really couldn't be any easier.

Programming your crystal isn't a requirement. The crystal will still function in all the ways we have talked about, such as raising vibrations, clearing a room of negative energy and amplification of positive energy, among other things.

However, if you are going to request the help of a crystal for something specific (during meditation for astral travel or to contact Angels or Spirit Guides, for example), you will get better results if you program your crystal with that specific intent.

Even if your crystal is just going to be used in a general way to uplift the energy in an environment or to help decrease negativity, it is still helpful to program it as such.

Programming your crystal allows you and your crystal to work together toward a clearly focused goal.

Record Keepers are crystals that have pre-programming in them. This kind of programming is the "non-erasable" (a read-only) kind, so you don't have to worry about accidentally clearing a crystal of valuable hidden information. As with a folder that contains read-only files, you still may be able to add files to the folder, but you cannot erase or modify the read-only files. So it is possible to program a Record Keeper crystal with a request for assistance entirely different than the information that may be present in its hidden "read-only" programming. There is plenty of room for all the programming you might want to add, as well as the pre-recorded information.

However, even though there is room on a crystal for us to make many programs or requests, it is best to program a crystal with a single intention; the focus is better that way.

You may worry that in the beginning you might program a crystal the "wrong" way. With programming as with cleansing, intent is more important than content. You really can't do anything wrong with a crystal if your intent is good. You can't mess it up or cause irreparable damage with your programming.

You might wonder, "What if someone wanted to program a crystal for evil purposes?" What happens then? Knowing that crystal isn't simply an inanimate tool, like a hammer or screwdriver, those with negative intent (incarnate or discarnate) can't use a crystal in just any way they choose.

For example, an inanimate tool such as a hammer can be used for either positive or negative intent. The hammer doesn't have a say in how it is used. You can use a hammer on a nail or you can use a hammer on someone's skull with very different results, depending on your intent. By comparison, crystals are sentient Beings of Light. They don't function like the hammer.

To illustrate, we are agreed that an empty box with a lid on it would be dark inside, right? If you take the box into a lighted room and open it up, it won't make the room darker. The light will fill the box and the dark will disappear, so even if someone *tried* to interject dark into a crystal, it simply won't take.

Here is an important piece of information for every one of us to remember: Because crystals are sentient, ancient, and wise Beings of Light, unlike humans, they cannot ever be tricked or coaxed into harmful uses. They simply cannot be accessed or programmed for desires that do not serve their purpose of teaching and expanding Light and Love.

The first step in preparing to program your crystal is CLEARING.

Clearing is erasing prior programming.

Remember, *cleansing* erases prior energy signatures but *clearing* erases prior programming.

I would compare clearing to the deleting of erasable files. Your computer still works just as it did, anything saved to memory (such as Record Keepers) stays in place, you are just erasing the temporary files that were added. When you're done with this particular file (which in crystal-speak is a program), then you erase and start new.

What I'm attempting to do with these file and memory comparisons is to better help you understand crystals and how they function regarding programming and memory.

We already talked about how crystals compare to humans, including how they also compare to computers. They store memories, senses, feelings and factual information, just like we do. However they are more like computers in that they are able to hold information for an indefinite period of time; so, too, is the information more accurate than when compared to the subjectivity of humans.

Crystals are still sentient beings; cleansing, clearing and programming don't affect this aspect of your crystal.

Intent is even more important when clearing than when cleansing because clearing is a more focused mental endeavor. Remember, when you *cleanse* a crystal, it is a general energy washing; however, when you *clear* a crystal, it is comparable to focused, intense erasing.

You are intending that any prior programming be erased while asking the crystal to please clear itself. You also let it know that your intent is to program it with something new.

To clear, you start the same way as when you cleanse, before *adding focus and specific intent.*

Clearing requires more focus, so I would choose one of the more immediate methods like smoke or running water that doesn't involve overnight basking.

Be thankful and respectful.

Always keep in mind the sentience of your crystal friend, knowing that this is a shared endeavor. It is not an employer/employee relationship in which you tell the crystal what to do and it does it.

Many books and how-to articles imply that crystals are simply tools here for our use. They are tools, yes, but so, too, are our friends and teachers tools. We enter into a co-creative contract with these people every time we interact. It is the same with our crystal friends and teachers.

It seems to me, that as humans, we are taught to view... well... really anything non-human... as somehow "less than" we are; as tools for our exploitation.

The truth is the only difference between the Crystal People and our human friends is that we need to remember that the crystals are ancient beings.

I have said this before but it bears repeating; they deserve our infinite respect, love and gratitude. Just as it isn't a *requirement* that our human friends or teachers help us, it isn't a requirement that the Crystal People help us. They *choose* to help us; that needs to remain in the forefront of our minds.

OK! Now let's talk about how to PROGRAM your crystal.

First of all, your program should focus on a single desire. You intend that this crystal help you with "X", not "X and Y and Z."

It isn't because a crystal can't do more than one thing at a time; it is because *we* can't (at least not successfully).

Have you ever heard of the computer acronym GIGO? It stands for *garbage in, garbage out*.

If we are scattered in our desire, the crystal will help us as much as it can, but unless we are focused on a specific outcome, it can't help us to get there. It isn't because the crystal isn't capable of doing so without our input; it is because to do so would take away our free will and subsequently, water-down the lessons we are here to learn.

Each crystal that we are programming is helping to pull us into this now moment regarding each particular program or desire.

If you have several areas you need help with, feel free to enlist the help of more than one crystal.

For example: "This crystal is for help with astral travel," "This crystal is for helping me to maintain focus in weight loss," "This crystal is for connecting to my higher Self," and so on. If you only have one crystal, work on one item at a time, being sure to clear and re-program your crystal between each issue.

Once you have decided what your goal is, the next step will be choosing which crystal wants to partner with you in order to get that help. How do you choose? I would start with intuition and see where you are guided.

Whether you have a lot of crystals or only one, there is nothing wrong with using what you already have.

If you do have several crystals from which to choose, lay them out and ask them “I need help with this. Who would like to help me?” Don't just grab one; stop and listen. Feel them with your energy (or listen, or see, depending on your connection language: your “clair”).

Determine to which one you are being pulled.

If you aren't getting a clear answer (or aren't able to decipher the answers from the crystals), then look to their differing characteristics.

For example, if you want to learn math, you would need to find a math teacher. Likewise, if you know you want assistance with astral travel, seek out a Faden crystal. If you know you want to connect with your partner or potential partner, seek a Twin or Soul Mate. If you need to boost optimism and hope, look for a Rainbow crystal.

These crystals can help you with other things as well, but these areas are their specialty.

In other words, if you don't feel as though you are getting a clear response from the crystals you asked, then seek out a “specialist” known to be skilled in the area in which you need help.

Using the math teacher example again, maybe you have an auto mechanic friend who is fantastic at math and makes it clear that she really wants very much to help you improve your math ability.

So even if she is not “officially” a math teacher, you trust her intent and contract with her to work together on your math skills.

On the other hand, if you ask all of your friends and family and no one steps forward to be your personal math teacher, then it's time to find yourself a certified teacher that you know loves math and wants to work with you.

Okay, so now you have decided which crystal you want to assist you with your desire (program). The next thing you should do is *cleanse* and *clear* that crystal.

Cleanse it in case it has picked up residual energy in the environment since the last cleansing, and then clear it of any prior programming.

To recap, you may cleanse your crystal with running water, sage, incense or smoke or in a bed of herbs or dry salt.

I like to cleanse and clear my crystal at the same time, using the same method. What I mean by this is, whatever method I choose, I begin with the intention of *cleansing* (eliminating prior energy), and then shift my focus to *clearing* (eliminating prior programs).

Technically you could choose to cleanse with one of the slower, basking-type methods such as an overnight nap in herbs or dry salt, and then follow up the next day with a focused clearing method employing water or smoke, etc. The focus here, again, is on intent.

Remember crystals are old; even if *you* haven't programmed this crystal, someone might have in the past, and so it is always good to erase the blackboard and ensure that you are starting with a clean slate. It is also demonstrating to the crystal that you are present and focused on your desired outcome.

Also, if it is a crystal you have had for a while, you might have programmed it (intentionally or unintentionally) and forgotten.

I had this happen when I was first starting on my journey with the crystals. It is when I was just beginning to visit the crystal mines frequently and my cancer had just returned.

Sit back and I will tell you the story.

I had a wonderful masculine point that was nearly optically clear. I loved this point. It fit well in my hand and I carried it in my pocket.

A dear old friend of my grandparents died. He had been in his 90's. I really hadn't known him for a long time, but he was an artist and we made an instant heart connection when we met. We shared laughter, stories and favorite painting techniques.

I was very sad when he passed. I went to his funeral and my crystal was with me. We attended the service at his graveside and when I walked by, I touched the top of his coffin with my crystal.

To be honest, it had become my intention to leave my crystal there with him, to maintain a connection of sorts. At the last minute, I changed my mind and put my crystal friend back in my pocket.

When it came time to let go, while I wanted to share my crystal with my friend, at the same time, I couldn't bear to part with it.

Fast forward several months. I had continued to carry that crystal everywhere with me.

I was just learning about programming and I decided I wanted to program a crystal. I was also learning how to meditate and use crystals for assistance with focus.

Remember this was before I really knew anything about crystals.

When I was deciding which crystal to begin with, I thought to myself, "who better than this special crystal friend who has been everywhere with me?"

So I put my special crystal in my hand, I got very quiet, and still, and focused my intent (the program).

As I was sending my intent out my arm and into the crystal, in the quiet stillness, coming back up my arm and into my consciousness, I *heard* and *felt* a voice say three words very clearly "I. AM. DEAD."

Oh! Holy cow! I dropped my crystal like a hot potato. I'm telling you that this scared the holy bohonkus out of me!

I don't usually hear things; remember I am a "feeler." So when I *heard* as well as felt this I was *completely* freaked out! I put my crystal away and decided not to finish programming it that day.

Of course, the experience didn't harm me in any way, but it *did* slow my progress with programming crystals in the immediate future.

On looking back, it didn't take me long to figure out what had happened.

My *intent* all through the funeral service had been to leave my crystal to maintain a connection with my friend. (My intent became a program.)

My emotions were so intense when I was at the funeral that when I touched my crystal to my artist friend's coffin, I believe they connected and the program was set.

Obviously, since my emotions were intense, even *without* the unintended programming, my crystal should have been cleansed as soon as I got home from the funeral.

When the crystal and my (now-deceased) friend connected, the crystal was programmed. Even though I assumed it was clear of any prior programming (after all, I dug the crystal myself, I had been the only human it had been in contact with), it still should have been cleared before programming.

This story should serve as a gentle, but necessary, reminder on why you should always, *always* clear a crystal with focused intent before programming it. Never make assumptions.

Cleanse and clear, cleanse and clear; it is very important.

So, you've cleansed and cleared and are about to program. The next thing you should do is familiarize yourself with your crystal.

Remember what you did when you were just meeting your crystal? Sit with it and check in with how you are feeling before you pick it up. Then notice how you feel with the crystal in your hand, etc. It is important to do all of this again.

You may have already done that with this crystal; that's okay. It may take less time than it did in the beginning; but it is still an important step. You still need to reconnect, and the best way to do that is with the check-in.

Proper sitting posture is important. Sit with your spine straight with your feet flat on the floor.

Don't forget to clear your mind. You want to focus on this one thing that you need assistance with, so you don't want to boggle your crystal up with mind chatter.

Connect your head to the heavens and your feet to the earth. Now ground yourself while remaining uplifted.

Programming is usually best done with your crystal in your dominant hand. You are going to send your desire from your mind, feel it in your body, and send it out your arm and hand, into the crystal.

Your crystal should be in your dominant hand because your non-dominant hand is receptive. Your right hand is dominant if you are right handed, left if you are left handed.

You are *sending* this program *into* the crystal.

You may use the crystal in your receptive hand after it is programmed. However, there are always exceptions.

Next, imagine your desire as complete (see yourself successfully astral travelling, see yourself at the weight you want to be, etc.). This is the usual "Law of Attraction" philosophy. Visualize and feel yourself not in the wanting and waiting stage, but in the *completed* stage.

Your crystal can connect you to all times, past, present and future. Be in the NOW with your desire complete and successful. This is what you are programming into your crystal.

Here is a recap:

- Ask the crystal's permission to program it for a specific task;

- Cleanse and clear your crystal in preparation for programming;

- Determine your intention and hold it in your mind in clarity;

- Check in, first without the crystal and then with it in your hand;

- Move the crystal to your dominant hand;

- Listen carefully for any guidance you receive;

- Be in the moment of successful completion of your desire. Pour this feeling into the crystal. Whatever it is you are programming: see it, feel it, taste it. Send all of this into your crystal so it can remind you of this feeling when you are in need of either a boost or additional assistance with this particular task.

- The final step: when you are finished with your positive visualization and focused intent, indicate to the crystal that you are finished. Let it know that you are ready for it to take over. Thank it for its assistance in helping you complete this task, whatever the task may be.

Remember that your crystal is present in all times. Your crystal is already there with your successful self in the future. The crystal can “see” that you have already completed whatever task you programmed it to help you achieve.

Ask your crystal to hold that vision for you until you have achieved it or until you have changed your direction. Ask that it remind you when you need a boost.

Ground out the energy and put your crystal somewhere special. For example, you may put it in your pocket, or make jewelry out of it, or perhaps it is meant to go by your bedside. It will depend on what your purpose was; you will know what is right.

Reinforce your program periodically.

Remember that you will need to cleanse (not clear) your crystal at least monthly at the proper phase of the moon for your purpose. Cleanse it outdoors under the moon if you can; if you can't, then use your intent to cleanse it indoors (remember the Gulag example).

Reinforce your program (remind yourself and the crystal what your desire is) when you take it outdoors for cleansing.

As a reminder, a new moon growing to full moon energy is for programs of things that you want to increase. By comparison, a full moon shrinking to new moon energy is for programs of things you want to decrease.

Remember, while you may *cleanse* in a different moon phase, it is always appropriate to *charge* your crystal in the energy of the full moon, even for crystals which are programmed to assist you with decrease. Depending on your program, you may have it outside twice a month; one time basking in the waning or waxing moonlight to *cleanse*, and the next time, during the night of the full moon to *charge*.

So what about healing?

You've heard that crystals are wonderful healers. How does that work?

We're going to spend a whole chapter on that very subject, so I'll be seeing you there!

Crystals have been assisting people with healing for as long as there have been people who needed curing.

The ancient cultures of Atlantis and Lemuria have already been discussed.

Shaman and medicine people all over the globe have used crystals (and continue to do so).

It has been the same for ancient Egyptians; likewise for countless other cultures and people.

While this brief list is in no way exhaustive, it does serve to give you an idea of how long crystals have been assisting with the healing of humankind and the planet.

As Lightworkers, we use crystals for healing.

Until the entry of these new earth energies, as we discussed earlier, they have most often been described in books, blogs, or lectures simply as tools to use and set aside at will.

I am hoping to change your mind about this one fact.

Crystals are sentient beings, and they are *assisting us* with our own healing. They do not heal us.

We won't wake up magically one day after acquiring a Golden Healer (or whatever other type of crystal we adopt; you fill in the blank) and discover we are cured of this illness or that malady. We have to take part in the healing process and take responsibility for our own healing (or lack, thereof).

Don't get me wrong, I believe the possibility is there, and it could certainly happen. However, just as with all of the other topics we have discussed, I view healing as a co-creative endeavor between the crystals and ourselves.

There are many good reasons to include working with crystals as an adjunct to our ongoing healing process. One excellent reason is that there are no negative side effects.

You may not believe that they work, or you may think that maybe they do, but you aren't quite sure. I will tell you this: it can't hurt to try.

Remember, crystals cannot ever *harm* you, even if you don't believe they can *help*.

The worst case scenario is that your lack of belief, and, therefore, insincere intention, limits their ability to help you, but the best case scenario is that they may, indeed, help without you even realizing it.

Always keep in mind that you are responsible for your own wellbeing. You can't neglect yourself in the healing process and then expect the crystals to magically heal you while you sleep. However, they may help while you sleep IF you are taking an active role with your Higher Self, Spirit Guides, and others *during* that sleep.

I know I have said this already, and will probably say it yet again, but it is a vitally important concept to grasp.

It is a co-creative process; the crystals aren't healing anything on their own; they are here to *assist you* in your own healing process.

There are many ways we can use the assistance of crystals in our personal healing process: headaches, nausea, chakra balancing, increasing one's vibrations, boosting the immune system and sharpening one's focus, to name just a few. Crystals can bring us light, increase our optimism, and even give us energy.

The possibilities are as limitless as your imagination.

It is important to remember to cleanse your crystal after each healing session, because it is working hard on your behalf. Don't forget it is sometimes necessary to cleanse it DURING the healing process.

Remember the Tabby crystal that I used on my stomach for nausea during chemotherapy? It had to be cleansed several times during each healing session.

The intent was that the crystal would absorb the disquiet as it was rubbed in a circular motion. It would begin to feel “sticky” energetically when it was “full,” and I would shake it off frequently during the session. It was very helpful and repeated cleansing was a key to the success.

Formal knowledge, or special training, is not necessary when you decide to do healing work on yourself with your crystal. You don't need a certificate or diploma. You don't need to have someone tell you that you are now worthy of working with your crystal friends.

Crystals are here for everyone. All that is required is that you listen to, and follow, your inner guidance as well as the guidance of the crystal.

If you choose to assist others with their healing process, it is not necessary that you have a diploma, degree, or formal training, but it is ethical to tell them that you do not if they assume that you do.

It's also important to tell the person you're working with that they are responsible for their own healing, and that you are simply there to assist them, as are the crystals (which is what we talked about earlier).

Crystals are a wonderful adjunct to Reiki and other energy work modalities.

As discussed earlier, you may have only one crystal or you may have several; they may range in size from very small to very large.

If you only have one crystal, then do what you need to do!

Again, there are no hard and fast “rules” that you must follow. There is no end to the possibilities and combinations that you may find useful. It will depend on your personal choice and what you are led to do.

Just remember that each task is a separate program (for example healing, anti-nausea, or raising energy).

You may choose to program the crystal for assistance with a particular healing session in which you intend to cover many areas; this is “fudging” a bit on the “one program per crystal” suggestion, but remember it is intent that is important. Also your healing (no matter how many areas that may cover in a session) is still the main focus.

If you do something differently from what you may have read in a book and/or are told by someone, that doesn't make it incorrect. Listen to your inner guidance, and you can never go wrong!

Every illness or disease that you can think of is fair game when considering crystals as an adjunct to your healing.

Along that line, I want to address a controversy that has persisted for at least as long as I have been using crystals in the healing work on myself, and that controversy involves working with crystals on someone with cancer.

In the beginning, people would get wide-eyed and say to me, "NO! Never use crystal during cancer therapy because crystal amplifies energies, and this will cause the cancer to grow and spread. Never use crystal for cancer!"

I can see how people might misunderstand and think in this way, but crystals aren't going to increase the growth of cancer cells unless your intention is that they will.

Even then, it isn't the crystal causing the growth, but your intention.

This is an important concept to wrap your head around.

I will repeat it; healing work is a co-creative endeavor. That means both you and the crystal must be on the same page in order to cause a change. Your intention must be clear and the energy you lend to the crystal is of the utmost importance.

If you don't engage with the crystal, waving it around with no connection between you and it, not very much is going to happen.

If you take the crystal with some mad scientist idea and decide you want to grow someone's cancer or cause destruction and mayhem, remember you both have to be on the same page.

Crystals simply aren't ever going to get on that page with you.

Remember my question about what happens if you open the lid on a box in a room filled with light?

The dark isn't going to stay in the box. The light will shine in there and now you have a box full of light.

If you still feel uncertain about using crystal during cancer treatment (or during ANY particular treatment), then *do not use it*. It's as simple as that.

Remember our mantra: *intent not content*.

If you are unable to come on board with your intent, then don't do it. Always follow your own intuition and guidance. Intuition and guidance trumps any information gained from an outside source in all circumstances.

Specifically, then, how would a person use crystals along with other healing modalities (alternative or traditional)? We know they are very helpful with meditation and focus.

I used my crystals whenever I was having a procedure or treatment. They were good company and they also helped me to enter a deep meditative state so I was more out of body than in it.

You can use them as we discussed earlier for positive visualization to assist you in entering a space in this now moment in order to access your future healed self.

This assists in the Law of Attraction. What we put out with our vibrations we receive back. Positive visualization is imperative in the healing process of any illness.

Remember, using crystals for assistance isn't a magic pill; you still have to do the work.

This might be a good time to briefly address my beliefs about soul contracts.

Sometimes an illness is introduced into our energy field for a specific purpose (in my case, it was to pull me back onto the right path, my soul path, after I had gotten so far off-track).

The reasons will be as varied as there are people on the planet.

I view some illness like a hole in our path that was pre-planned before we even arrived on the Earth-plane in order for us to experience a valuable lesson.

Other illnesses are simply a hole in the path that we stepped into accidentally or were shoved into by some outside force.

Whatever the reason for being in the hole, we are there.

Please understand, I'm not saying that if you are ill, it is your fault, you asked for it and too bad for you. I'm only suggesting that if we happen to find ourselves in a hole, the best next step is to find a way out of it.

Sometimes the only way out of a hole is to transition to the next level.

There is no negative judgment in that.

Most often if you look back, valuable life lessons have been learned through the catalyst of illness. They were not easy lessons and it wasn't an easy process, but they were valuable lessons none-the-less.

Again, please don't take this as judgment or lack of sympathy for the hardships you or your loved ones may be experiencing; it's just a perspective on illness that I gained from going through my own.

Okay! Let's get back to healing.

You are already aware that crystals are helpful to amplify energy. So what better assistance than in the amplification of healing energy such as Reiki?

Crystals help us to both focus and direct our energy; they also serve to raise our vibration, which can be most useful in assisting with mood elevation. I know for me, when I was at the crystal mine, even at my sickest, I always felt better. Even if it was only emotionally better, that elevated my mood, which, subsequently, made my physical body feel better.

When you are depressed, everything hurts more and gloom easily turns to inky black doom. This can lead to an increase in pain, and the cycle continues.

Crystals can help us to spiral upward instead of downward. In this way they help us to raise our mood. Raising one's mood helps with the immune system.

When you are in a better space vibrationally, your body can function as it was meant to.

Crystals, then, can assist you in manifesting health and wellness by attracting higher vibrational energies into your aura.

Remember, too, that crystal can be used as a conduit to your higher Self or Universal Truth. Some people may refer to this Oneness as God or Goddess, The Creator, All That Is, or whatever term fits your personal belief.

Remember, crystals can be used as bridges to other realms so that you may access Spirit Guides, Angels and even extraterrestrials.

If you don't believe in these things, well, then I don't suppose you will be contacting them.

If, however, you believe the purple Snuffleuphagus exists in another, higher realm, pick up your crystal telephone and make that call!

Having access to your own personal guidance, in whatever form that takes, can be helpful to your healing process.

While crystals may be used in many ways, not all of them require actually holding the crystal.

They can be placed in grids, jewelry, wands, or pendulums; they can be used to emanate light through your connection (the etheric cord).

The layout of such grids, or the creation of wands, pendulums or jewelry will depend on the termination of a point (clusters, single terminations versus double, etc) and we'll get into that later.

For now, let's discuss the many different grids that can be made with the assistance of our crystal friends.

Crystal Grids

A crystal grid is a layout of crystals placed around a person, (in which you want to affect a change), or a place, (in which you want to maintain a vibration).

You might place a grid around a person for healing or protection.

Grids can be placed around a room, a house, or property, for energy amplification, protection, positivity and shielding.

Pets and plants may also benefit from crystal grids. Crystals are placed in a specific pattern surrounding the place, person, animal or plant in question.

Programming the crystals is necessary for your grid to work properly.

You may choose to program them for any of the reasons I mentioned above. Again, the possibilities of uses for crystal grids are as limitless as your ideas.

I'm going to describe a few possibilities, and then you take that knowledge and use your imagination. The sky is the limit here!

Intuition is of utmost importance in the process of gridding.

If you simply feel, or know, that a particular crystal needs to be facing in a certain direction, or needs to be included in the grid, then by all means, listen to that guidance. You may be receiving it from your Higher Self, a Spirit Guide, or more likely, from the crystal itself.

It may be that inner voice whispering, "pssst... hey buddy… pssssst… hey buddy! Put me this way or put me on that corner or put me next to this other guy."

Follow the guidance you are given. You don't have to know why you are doing it, you don't have to have this all planned out by degrees and angles and quadrants. Your gut is your best guide; listen to it.

You may select empathic crystals or intact crystals for placement in your grids. There are no rules about which types you must use.

I tend to use empathic points and clusters if they are going to be somewhere that I'm not going to see them or have access to them.

For example, I have empathic clusters built into the subfloor of my bedroom and buried around the property. The energy is still there and it is a great way to put the less aesthetically "beautiful" crystals to great use.

I cringe because all crystal is beautiful and I feel like a skunk implying that this crystal might be more appropriate to put where you aren't going to see it; that's not my intent.

I do know myself, however, and if I put a ten-inch optically clear channeling crystal in my subfloor, I might wish, at some point, that I had access to it so we could do some different work together.

It would be wise to choose a crystal for gridding that you're not going to want to take a pickaxe to the floor of your bedroom to get to at some later date.

Permanent grids versus temporary grids are also a determining factor in crystal choice.

In a temporary grid it is ok to use crystals that you might want to use later for something else.

For example the ten-inch optically clear Channeler I was just joking about might be perfect for a temporary grid.

The grid under my bedroom obviously is meant to be a permanent grid, as is the grid around my property, where crystals are buried. These crystal grids are meant to stay in place. I'm not moving these grids.

Less permanent grids would be the crystals lining the flowerbeds and ringing the trees. They are probably there at least semi-permanently, unless one moves the flowerbed or decides to re-arrange.

Another semi-permanent grid might be on top of your bird's cage or around the bed of your pet.

An example of a temporary grid might be one you place around a person during a healing session.

Access is the key.

You will need to periodically cleanse and reinforce your grids. The cleansing in the cave or the gulag example from earlier will come in handy for this.

You won't have to dig up your grid or tear up the floor of your bedroom; you simply touch in and intend that your grid is cleansed. This checking-in also reinforces the connection and keeps the grid running.

Let's discuss specific ways to make a permanent grid.

You can grid a room. If you are as lucky as I was, you might be present when a room is being built; this is when you can place your grid beneath the subfloor, making it much easier to sweep and vacuum later!

If you have this beneath-the-floor opportunity, you may choose to place one crystal in each corner, or one right in the center of the room.

You can put as many or as few as you want, as large or small as you have. You can use clusters, points or chunks, it doesn't matter.

Intent, as always, is paramount.

While we're on the topic of permanent grids, an important thing to take into consideration is how you are personally affected by the energy of crystals.

I am on an even keel with their vibration (we mesh quite nicely), so I have never had this problem; however, I have a dear friend who did have this problem at one point, so it bears mentioning.

She was unable to wear a crystal necklace for long periods because the energy gave her a headache. Being in a room full of crystals made her buzz and react like she'd just ingested a pot of coffee.

If you have this sort of reaction to the higher vibration of crystal, it might not be a good idea to grid your bedroom. Instead, you might choose to grid the kitchen or the living room, but not your sleeping area.

I have been living with thousands of crystals in my living space, in my bedroom and closets for coming up on twenty years.

I am accustomed to the vibration and fare quite well.

This may not be true for you, though, so be cautious of this knowledge when you position your grids, especially if it is a permanent choice, like building them into a room.

A semi-permanent or temporary grid can always be moved if it's making you crazy. If you've already placed crystals in a permanent grid and you find they *are* making you crazy, all is not lost. You can touch in with the crystals in your grid and request that they lower their energetic output for you.

You can also make a permanent grid around your house or around your entire property. You may bury the crystal at the corners of your house, under each window, or near the doors. For your property, choose the four corners and space along the fence line if it is big.

If you have a large property (like acres of land) you can make a small scale replica and grid that to represent your property. To do this, you would energetically ask each crystal to be present over a specific area.

Again, let me hammer this home: Intent is the key.

You can also layer your grids. You may grid a room, then your house, your plants and trees and then your property.

A room may be gridded for positivity and your house for protection and the holding of a high vibration.

You may build a grid for your plants and trees so that they grow and thrive. Grids can be placed to attract fairies and elementals, if that is your intention.

Your property can be gridded for protection, love, healing and positivity.

All of these grids in place at once is what we refer to as layering grids.

Don't forget to cleanse the crystals periodically and touch base to reconnect and reaffirm your intention within the grid.

Use your etheric cord connection to reinforce your grids. This means you will need to connect with the crystals before you make the grid.

You don't have to hold each one and go through the entire process individually. Select the ones you want to use in your grid, and connect with them as a group.

You will be working with them collectively, so this is a better idea than individually connecting, anyway.

After cleansing and clearing, visualize the intent and goal that you have for the grid.

Next, ask the crystals to hold that intention for you; that is programming the grid.

Finally, offer your thanks and gratitude for their continued assistance.

Healing grids obviously are different than home or property grids, but they work the same way. First, you select the crystals you would like to help you in your healing session.

Do this either by pure intuition or by the configuration of the crystal, as discussed earlier. You may have a set of crystals you use exclusively for healing work. Connect with them and request their help in the healing session with Person X.

You can also lay a grid for yourself. For your healing grid, you may place the crystals around a bed, recliner or even on the floor. Just be sure to lay them out wherever you are going to be most comfortable.

State your intention to the crystal, see yourself or the person in the grid in their highest light.

If you wish, along with assistance from the Crystal People, you can ask for assistance from the Creator, Spirit Guides and Angels.

Lay the crystals around the person in whatever way you feel led, and then let the person "cook."

Keep in mind the direction of the energy that is flowing out of your crystal points. Imagine them as arrows, the termination being the arrow point. Whichever direction the arrow is pointing is the direction the energy will flow.

Double Terminated crystals flow in both directions.

You may choose to lay the grid of crystals right on the person, or around their body.

If it's a grid for yourself, it might be easiest to lay them around you so that the ones you have placed don't fall off as you place more.

Grids can be used in distant healing, as well.

If you have a friend that is in need of healing or protection or positivity or … (fill in the blank), you can make a grid for them where you are.

Get a picture of the person, or something which represents them, and put it in the center of the grid.

Select your crystals, cleanse and clear them, and program them with the particular intent you have for this grid.

Visualize your friend in their highest light, healed and whole in this NOW moment. Ask the crystals to hold that energetic signature for you.

The pattern in which you place the crystals is up to you. You might place them in a starburst pattern, all facing in toward the person if they are in need of energy. You might place them in a starburst pointing out if they are trying to rid themselves of something. You might place them in a circle, arrow point to base for protection.

If you have a lot of double terminated points, you could lay them in a starburst around the person so the energy would both flow into and out of them.

Follow your inner guidance. There are no rules. These are just suggestions to prime your pump of ideas.

Animals also benefit from grids.

My umbrella cockatoo, Daisy, is particularly high strung. She was going nutty from hormones and frustration because her mate was not responding to her advances. Guess who her “mate” is? That's right, it's me. It makes for an awkward situation. I was starting to approach my wits end because she was so nervous, jittery and cranky. There was really nothing I could do to help her. Well, Crystal People to the rescue! I placed a grid on her cage.

In Daisy's case, I choose to use amethyst because of its calming energies. I chose amethyst *clusters* in particular because they were large enough not to fall through the bars on the top of her cage.

I cleansed, cleared and programmed the crystals to assist Daisy to be calm and happy. I asked her Spirit Guides, and any helpers that may be present who work with animals, birds in particular, to please help.

I placed the amethyst clusters on each of the four corners of her cage, said a small prayer and she became less cranky and noticeably calmer.

Recently her frustration level has been increasing. I added a Selenite oval to the center of the four-point Amethyst grid, to introduce soothing angelic energies and to help the Amethyst remain cleansed.

The crystal on Daisy's cage is an example of a semi-permanent grid. I leave the crystals on her cage, but I can move them if and when I need to. I touch-in with the crystals daily when I put her to bed and cleanse and charge them as needed. Daisy's grid is also a perfect example of using different crystal types as well as altering the grid as the situation warrants.

Just be sure to remember that gridding is a fluid endeavor.

As discussed earlier, you can do this with dogs, cats, even fish. Remember, though, that it is safest to put the crystal on the outside corners of your fish tank, not inside.

Any animal you have can benefit from your use of a crystal grid to help them. You just need to cleanse, clear, program and intend. It's as easy as that.

Once your grid is in place, if there has been a change in activity (such as a quarrel or something that has introduced negative energy into the environment, or intense healing work), cleanse your grid. If this seems daunting, remember you can cleanse your crystals without moving or touching them.

Be sure to reconnect and reinforce your grid on a regular basis. Remember to energetically charge your grid during the full moon while you're at it.

That should about cover the topic of gridding.

What about other ways we may enlist the assistance of our crystal friends?

How about wands and jewelry and pendulums? Oh my!

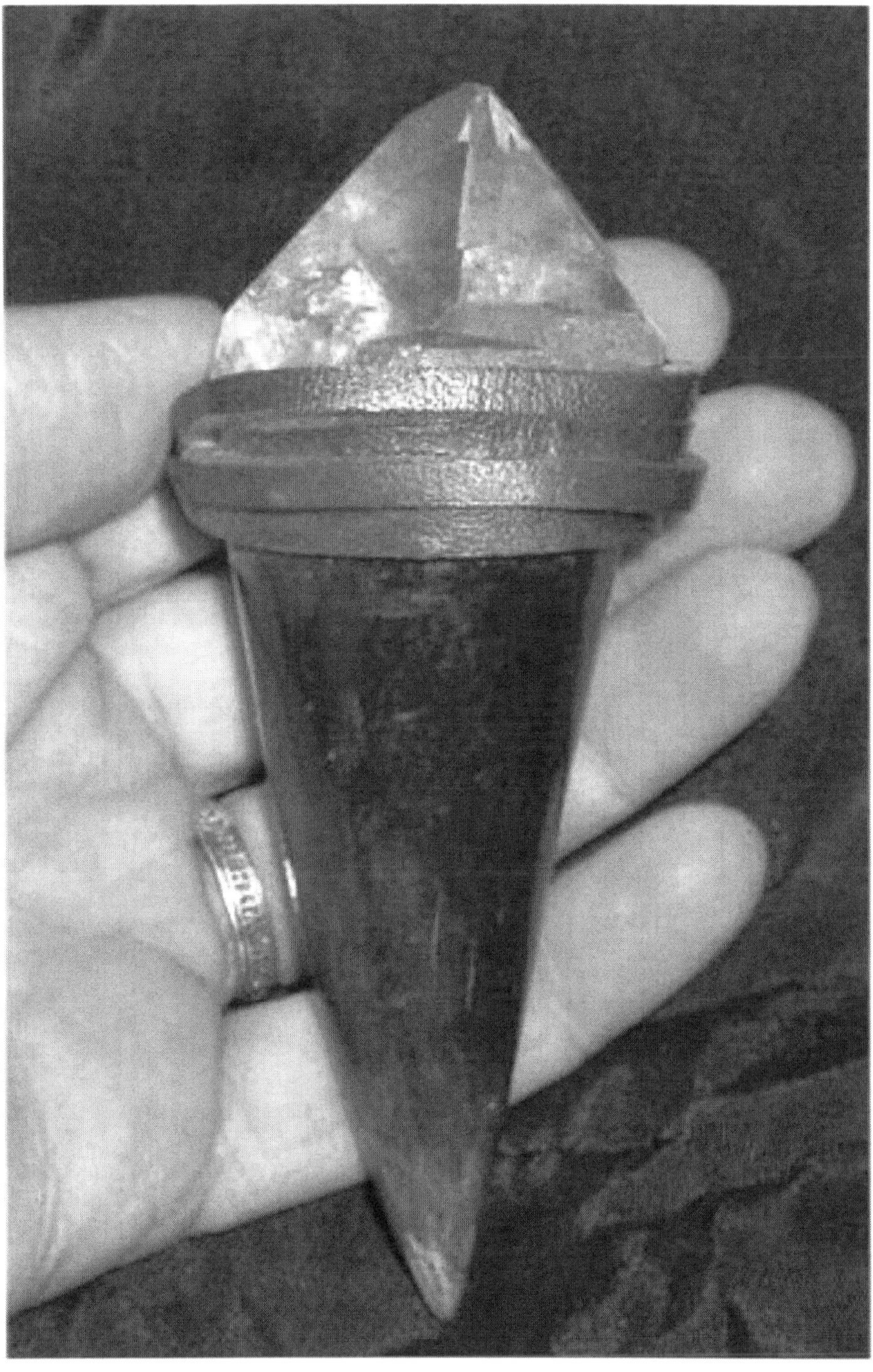

Other Uses

More practical, less intuition-centered choices are also available to you in employing the assistance of your crystal friends.

You may choose to incorporate them into tools.

People that have a more difficult time grasping the idea that crystals are sentient beings may have less trouble if they use a tool in which the energy of the crystal is intertwined.

Some examples of these tools are wands, pendulums and various types of jewelry.

All clusters or points are useful, even without focused intent or programming.

All of these different tool-based objects make great gifts for people that are not quite on board with the sentient idea, but do view crystals as helpful.

I'm not suggesting, in this chapter, that we are suspending the knowledge that crystals are ancient sentient beings.

I'm just providing you with some additional suggestions for people who aren't quite there yet.

Clusters may be placed in a home or office setting to increase the vibration and to absorb negative energy.

In the latter case, you need to be sure to cleanse your crystals frequently, especially after anything that may introduce negativity into the environment. Examples of this would be a visit from a person who is particularly negative, after a quarrel, or difficulties in the home or workplace.

Your points or clusters can be as benign looking as a paperweight. Your co-workers or family needn't know what you are using the cluster or point for; you know what it's doing and that's all that matters.

As stated above, it isn't necessary that you program a point or cluster for any specific purpose.

If you have a desire, it does help to program it with that intent, however. Program away if you feel led to do so; just don't feel obligated. You don't have to do anything to turn a crystal on. Crystals are “on” all the time, believe me!

As well as in the home or office as “decoration,” points or clusters may be placed at the bedside for any number of reasons.

They may assist in sleep or help with dream recall. You may place them there simply to increase the vibration in the room.

These are all examples of crystals being used in a “decorative” fashion while they are still working incognito.

Pocket crystals are great to have because you may easily carry them in a purse, or pocket, or wear them in a medicine pouch.

Just remember to connect and reinforce the connection with your crystal if you have programmed it for a specific purpose.

You may gift points or clusters with a specific intent.

The person to whom you gave the crystal doesn't have to believe in the energies; they are still present. They may simply experience a good feeling, and that's enough.

As we discussed earlier, crystals will amplify your energy and intent.

If you have fashioned a tool that incorporates crystals, then the energy and intent you put into that tool (or jewelry or decoration) will be amplified.

It is even better if you program the crystal as you make the tool.

Keep in mind the sentience of the crystal, asking their permission to incorporate them into your tool.

I occasionally get a “no” from a crystal with regards to a particular tool; this is actually part of the selection process you go though on deciding which crystal is best for the job.

It's not an indication that you shouldn't make the tool; it's simply a suggestion that there might be another crystal better suited for the situation.

Crystal wands can be made by applying crystals to different objects or they may simply be an unadorned crystal point.

It doesn't have to be "made" into a wand to function as one. However, if you decide to make a wand (or find one already made) it is helpful to know what it is you are looking at.

I make wands and am often asked by people "What are they for? How do you use them?"

They are used for focus and amplification, usually.

They can also be simply for decoration.

For example, I know lots of people who collect knives and hang them on their wall. They never use them for anything other than ornamentation.

The same can be true for wands. It depends on the person and their intent.

Wands can be used to direct or focus energy, to "cut" things energetically, to draw energy circles or send intentions.

These are just a few examples.

How would a person go about doing this, exactly?

Remember when we talked about gathering all your thoughts to program the crystal, sending them out your dominant hand and into the crystal?

When you use a wand, you are doing the same thing with your energy.

Mind you, your thought doesn't end with the crystal or wand; you send the energy out and through the wand to wherever, or whatever, you are doing.

A wand helps you to both focus your intent and then to direct that focus to a particular area, mainly because it amplifies the energy you are directing.

We've all heard about the young wizard Harry Potter, right? Until the students at Hogwarts learned how to focus their energy, their wands didn't work well.

It isn't the wand, but how you send your intent and focus through it. The crystal will help amplify that. You can pick up a stick, or a green bean, and use it as a wand. It's not in the tool, it's in the intention.

Add your intention to that of your crystal friend, and zowie, that green bean could become a mean, green, healing machine!

Crystal wands may be constructed out of nearly anything. You might use a stick, a glass rod, a seashell or a copper pipe. Copper is an excellent energy conductor.

Crystals may be wire wrapped onto the shaft, or hilt, of whatever material you choose, or you may use glue, leather or string.

The proper way to attach it will be whatever resonates for you. I always check with the crystal and see if there are any objections to using whatever method of affixing I have chosen. I like to use glue that won't yellow with time and have learned that Crafters Goop works quite well.

If you are opposed to using glue, then don't use glue; it's up to you and your crystal.

So many times we are instructed… *always* do this… *never* do that… this is the *only* way… this is the *right* way… that is the *wrong* way… If you come away with nothing else, I want you to know, with certainty, that whatever you *feel* is right, IS! If you feel led to use boogers and duct tape, do it! (However, don't expect that people will want to share use of your wand).

You may want to add other gemstones to your wand to lend different energetic qualities.

For example, you might use Selenite for Angelic energy.

Rose quartz can be used for love and Hematite can be used for grounding. The list is, literally, quite endless.

Okay, now let's switch gears and talk about pendulums.

Energy flow and vibration in crystal lends itself quite well for use as a pendulum.

The crystal is affixed to a chain of some sort by the method of your choice (wire wrap, glue, etc.).

Program the pendulum with your intent.

Perhaps you may program it for clarity.

A Generator or Merlin point makes an excellent pendulum because of the centrally located point and focused energy. A Dow would work very well as pendulum too. A centrally located point is ideal, but is not a requirement.

Making jewelry out of your crystal is a good way to ensure that your crystal is near at all times. Carrying crystal around may become a nuisance because you may not always have a pocket, purse or medicine pouch.

You can program your crystal jewelry, as well, for healing or energy or any other desire with which you need help.

When wearing crystal earrings, positioned at each side of your throat chakra, the crystal is also positioned by major arteries. In wearing two, you are afforded the added benefit of balanced energy. This is a great place for crystals programmed to help increase energy, to assist with healing, or for speaking your truth.

Crystals on necklaces are close to your heart and high heart chakra. You might program crystals in necklaces for love, truth, being open to possibilities and protection.

The choice of crystal configurations will vary according to your purpose. Some choices are Twin or Soul Mates for connection or Rainbows for hope and optimism.

Again the list is long, and the choice will depend upon your specific desire.

Just as with wands, you may add other minerals to your necklace to add extra energies, depending on their specific properties.

Double Terminated crystals in jewelry are handy for their ability to direct energy both up and down. They are good to connect all our chakras when worn lined up with our center.

Crystal jewelry, like plain points and clusters, may be gifted to people who don't necessarily believe in their “powers.” They will still benefit from the beauty, increased vibration and light inherent in the crystals themselves.

While we are on this topic, it is best to refrain from touching the jewelry, or tools, that belong to other people. Ask permission if you feel you simply must touch it. If the person says no, then respect their dcsire.

Personally, I don't feel that when people touch my crystal jewelry or tools that it causes any harm simply because I intend that it doesn't. This is not true for everyone, so it is always respectful to first ask permission.

Trees benefit from crystal “jewelry” as well.

I like to make mobiles out of driftwood. I wire wrap crystals and hang them from the wood. I then hang these in my trees. I believe the fairies and the tree spirits enjoy them.

There are many things you can make with crystals to increase energy, vibration and beauty.

Use the items you have created with your crystal to bring you into the present moment whenever you look at or use your tool, jewelry or decoration.

Through most of this chapter I have discussed tools which you have created and how to infuse them with your specific intent. This also applies to tools you purchase. Use the methods of cleansing, clearing and programming that you learned earlier.

Talking about making tools and jewelry has been fun!

Next, let's discuss the nuts and bolts of digging your own crystal.

I'll tell you where to go and the best time of year to dig.

We'll talk about what you need to bring and what to do with the crystal when you get home!

Digging Your Own Crystal

Crystal mining is really better described as crystal digging.

Digging is a more accurate term, especially for people like you and me, who are not actually mining.

Gathering is technically the process that I'll be describing, but to say you are gathering crystals invokes a picture of skipping through a meadow and picking flowers. This is not an accurate picture.

We've already discussed the details of the actual crystal mining process, so we won't go over that again.

What follows here will be a description of how to go about collecting your own crystals. While there are many other places in which you can pick up or collect your own crystals, we're just going to discuss collecting or digging crystals in Arkansas.

There are several mines from which to choose and I've added information on the current mines to the appendix at the back of the book.

Cool weather is the ideal time to go digging. In Arkansas, the most reliably cool weather occurs in the spring or fall. Of course, there are days during the winter that are mild and enjoyable and sometimes you might luck into a cool day in the summer.

Remember, in the actual mine area, you are up on a mountaintop with no trees around. You will be digging in full sun. Heat stroke is no joke. And on the other end of the spectrum, in the winter, the wind can be brutally cold. Add wet to that equation, and it can be truly miserable.

After you have chosen which mine to visit, you will arrive at the entrance. Usually there is a store, or another place, to check in. You will sign a liability release and pay your dig fee. The dig fees typically vary from $10 to $20 per person, per day for adults.

When you check in, the clerk will tell you where to park and where the entrance to the tailings is located.

Usually, they will tell you where the freshest tailings are; if they don't tell you, be sure to ask them.

Most Arkansas crystal mines are open every day except Christmas.

Typically, they let you dig from nearly dawn until dusk, and then they run you off with a stick (well, not really a stick, but they will run you off … nicely).

Some mines have fees based on an hourly rate, and they take you to the mine in their own truck. This is usually the exception to the rule, however.

If you have plans to dig and it happens to rain, don't worry. Other than it being incredibly messy and sloggy, some of the best crystal can be found during, or just after, a rain.

You are able to find more in the old tailings because the water washes the dirt off crystals that have been hiding from other diggers. To go the day after a really huge rain can provide you with some really great digging experiences.

But a serious reminder about this "better when it rains" scenario is not to forget about the sticky mess and the difficulty slogging through wet Arkansas red clay; it can be slippery and dangerous, and will also ruin your shoes and clothes.

In crystal digging, understanding the difference between fresh or "new" tailings versus old tailings is important. Keeping in mind the terminology I am discussing is new to you; I'll go over the terms again.

The giant hole where they do the actual mining is called the *pit*.

The piles of dirt, rock and crystal that they haul to the top are called the *tailings*.

The *new tailings* are the loads of dirt and rock that they have trucked up most recently.

The majority of the large mines operate nearly every day. If you are digging on a day in which they are actively working in the pit, the fresh tailings will be big piles of wet dirt, mud and clay. When you get your permit to dig, remember to ask them where they are dumping the new tailings.

If you're the sort who likes to dig through mucky mud, that's the area for you. It is also the area where you are most likely to find the really big crystals and clusters.

While some people prefer to work the new tailings, I prefer to walk the old.

What exactly does this mean?

The "old" tailings consist of the piles of dirt that have been there longer. They are made up of layer upon layer of what used to be the fresh tailings.

Periodically, a bulldozer will be used to move the dirt to make room for more material brought up from the pit. The dirt, rocks, and crystal get pushed up and up, so the old tailings can be quite high.

At the larger mines, generally you will find if the operators aren't actively working the pit, they are pushing the tailings around. This makes room for more material and also turns the dirt over to expose new areas for better digging.

I like to walk the old tailings because the energy seems softer. To me, the energy in the fresh tailings feels raw and exposed. Whether you prefer the fresh tailings or the old tailings will be something with which you will have to experiment; both have their ups and downs, pardon the pun.

Whichever area you decide on, crystal digging is a dirty process. Even when it's not wet, the red clay permanently discolors your clothes.

Wear something old that you don't mind getting stained. It is ideal if you have a pair of coveralls or overalls. When you are ready to pack it in and go home, you can strip off your dirty outer layer and ride home in relatively clean, dry clothes.

Of course, there are bathrooms at some (not all) of the mines, so you can change before you go home.

I find that I am usually too tired to change my clothes, and my truck is testament to this fact. You might want to put old towels or sheets over your seats if you are persnickety and don't want your vehicle to get all dirty, dusty and stained.

Sturdy shoes are a must, as well.

You will be climbing up and down large piles of dirt and rock. I've seen people come to dig wearing sandals or open toed shoes, and I don't recommend it. It isn't necessary to wear boots, any sturdy closed toe shoe is fine, but if you do have comfortable boots, all the better. You'll be the one not hobbling around because your shoes are full of rocks and dirt.

Hammers, picks and wedges are recommended by some of the more enthusiastic types, I don't recommend them at all, and it isn't only because it is hard work, and they are heavy, that I don't like using them.

The premise is to use them on the really large boulders that make their way out of the pit with partial veins still attached. Removing the crystal from the boulder is tempting, but it is usually best to leave it right there.

Here is why: smashing a crystal off the matrix is disappointing and brutal. Sadly, I have seen, and heard, this done over the years.

The sound is hideous (this is the brutal part); not only that, but crystal which has been unskillfully smashed off its matrix never has the luster that it did when it was still attached (this is the disappointing part).

If you are skillful and know what you are doing, you may be able to break the cluster off the sandstone without injuring it, but that isn't usually what happens. Normally, you end up with part of the cluster on the ground and part still on the rock, and you've irreparably damaged both.

One of the worst sounds I have encountered at the crystal mine is the relentless hammering followed by the sound of smashing, cracking crystal as it is being destroyed. The feeling in your gut which accompanies that horrible sound is infinitely worse.

Believe me, as tempting as it may be, it is best to leave it right there. The Crystal People, and your fellow crystal diggers, will thank you.

There is good news regarding large rocks with crystal attached. If you have the strength of Hercules and can get the rock from the tailings and into your car or truck, you're welcome to do so.

It is amazing that for the price of your permit, and providing you can get it into your vehicle, you really *can* take out anything you find in the tailings.

The heavier "mining tools" were recommended in the past because they used to let you go into the pit if they weren't working it on the day you went to dig.

Due to numerous safety hazards and OSHA regulations, they aren't allowing this practice anymore. So, my suggestion is to leave your hammer and bring a group of your strongest friends instead.

Lighter weight hand tools can be, well, handy! Garden trowels, a small hand shovel, even hemostats and tweezers.

You may be thinking, "Really, Genn! Tweezers?"

Well, if you have hemostats, you won't need tweezers. I never go the mine without my hemostats. If you don't know what they are, they're the scissor looking things with the alligator nose and locking grip. I like to clamp them to the front of my shirt so they are always at the ready. They are helpful in picking up really tiny crystals. They also can extend your reach up to a foot, which is nice when you're climbing the face of a steep hill. They are also good to use as diggers to loosen the dirt around crystals stuck in dry clay or packed dirt.

A three or four-pronged garden trowel can be very handy in both the old and new tailings.

Buckets of all sizes are invaluable. I tend to nest my buckets, large to small. I bring extras so that when I fill one bucket up I can leave it in the truck and start out fresh with an empty one. A five gallon bucket is tempting, but gets heavy quickly. If you have a little red wagon, bring it; they are to die for. If you don't have a wagon, use a smaller bucket.

I like to use the small mop buckets with the plastic tube on the handle. Inside this I will put a plastic coffee container and inside that a smaller container. The plastic containers that Crystal Light comes in are great; they have a lid and are the perfect size.

I know this sounds pretty fussy, and maybe it is, but it has worked for me over the years.

Usually inside at least one of these I will have a zip top plastic bag. Put your plastic bag in the container like you would put a plastic bag in a garbage can. When your container is full, you simply slide the bag out, zip it up and put it in your vehicle. This prevents you from having to pour your crystals out, possibly dinging or breaking them.

This leads me to the smallest containers I recommend. Pill or vitamin bottles are for especially small and/or fragile crystals. Lots of small bottles and containers and plastic baggies are a must. One set of stacking containers per digger is sufficient if you have plenty of plastic bags.

Speaking of using plastic bags in your containers like you would use garbage liners; it is best to plan to carry out everything you carry in. They usually have barrels on site for garbage. However, if you come prepared to take your garbage with you, there is no possibility of the wind blowing your trash out of the barrel and into the crystal mine.

I'm sure you and I view nature in the same manner. It is beyond disrespectful to see gum wrappers, cigarette butts, empty pop cans and bits of trash blowing about. If you are walking along and see someone else's trash, please do the crystals and Mother Earth a favor and pick it up.

Food and water are the other things you'll want to pack plenty of for your day at the mine. A picnic on the tailgate is a lot of fun. Plenty of drinking water is also essential, especially in the summer. Some of the mines have a store with vending machines on site, but not all do; be sure to ask.

We always bring more food than we need because usually there are hungry people who didn't think to bring food. Digging can be hungry work. Sharing with your fellow crystal enthusiast is good karma.

Not every mine has bathrooms on site. Some have portable toilets, the larger ones have "flushers," but it's best not to assume this. Check with the mine before you arrive. You might need to add toilet paper to your list of things to bring. If you're lucky and the mines do have a bathroom with flushing toilets and running water, no matter how tempting, please do them a favor and don't rinse off your crystals in the sink. The clay clogs the plumbing and can be a nightmare. Normally, there will be a special area with a pump or tubs full of water where you can do this.

Band-Aids, sun screen and other first aid items are always good to bring.

If you choose to dig in the new tailings, it is quite possible to cut yourself on the broken crystal hidden in the clay. Broken crystal is every bit as sharp as broken glass. I have been cut more times than I can count. If you aren't careful, it can cut you to the bone. Gloves are handy, but it can cut through them as well. Using a trowel instead of fingers is recommended.

Band-Aids come in handy; even when you're careful, you usually end up needing them. I will have to say that if you do cut yourself, the red clay in which the crystals grow works really well to stop the bleeding, and it promotes fast healing. Believe it or not, it is very beneficial. As a former nurse, I can't believe I'm suggesting that people put mud into their fresh wound. That having been said, I have done it and it works. Obviously, if this doesn't feel right for you, don't do it.

Now that we've discussed what to wear, what tools are essential, and the other intimate details of what to pack in your car, let's talk about what to look for in the tailings themselves.

In the new tailings, you will be looking for sticky masses of clay. At the majority of the mines I have been to, the clay is red. Some mines have different colors of dirt and clay, depending on the composition of the Earth. We'll just discuss the red clay, since it is in the majority, but keep in mind it may differ according to where you are. At any rate, the fresh tailings will look like wet, mushy mud and rocks. Most of the mud will be a dark brown color; some of it (if you're lucky) will be red clay.

Remember when we talked about the folding and faulting that created the mountains and the subsequent crevasses in which the crystal grew? Silt or mud filled in the gaps and acted as a sort of cushion for the clusters and points. This is the stuff you'll be looking for in the new tailings. The clay is red, sticky and gooey; it is clingy and hard to move.

What you'll be looking for inside the clay is anything black and shiny. The really clear points will appear black because you are seeing "through" them and into the dark of the inside. White looking areas in the mud are usually quartz matrix (the filler material with no points). Often there are points on the quartz matrix, so it is always a good idea to check.

Many a leaverite was brought home, not knowing until they were washed off if they were crystals or just chunks of matrix. What's a leaverite? That's a rock that when you see it you "leave 'er right" there. It's an old tongue-in-cheek rock hounding term. It's one of the first rock hounding words I learned because my grandparents considered most of the rocks I picked up to be leaverites.

Back to what to look for when you're digging; as I said, walking the old tailings is what I usually end up doing. In the beginning, I am always lured in by the promise of finding that really big, giant point or cluster in the fresh tailings. While this has yet to happen for me, I have seen it happen for many! However, after a usually unfruitful slog through the fresh tailings, the raw energy will become too much for me and I will end up strolling through the old tailings.

The same "shiny black" instruction is true for the old tailings as for the new. These need to be pried CAREFULLY out of the dirt with your trusty hemostats or garden trowel, being sure to scrape and loosen just the dirt *around* the crystal, but not the crystal itself.

The way I usually find crystal in the old tailings, however, is fairly easy to explain, but much harder to put into practice.

Have you ever seen those hologram posters? After getting your eyes focused, a picture suddenly emerges from what previously looked like just a bunch of splotchy colors.

Finding crystal can be like this. The splotchy colors are represented by dirt and rocks, the hologram is the crystal. You have to get your eyes set and scan the ground. If the sun is shining, that's all the better, because a flash of light here or there will alert you to where to center your gaze. If your focus is correct, a crystal may emerge. Your mind might register just the dirt, but with practice, right where you were looking, there is a crystal.

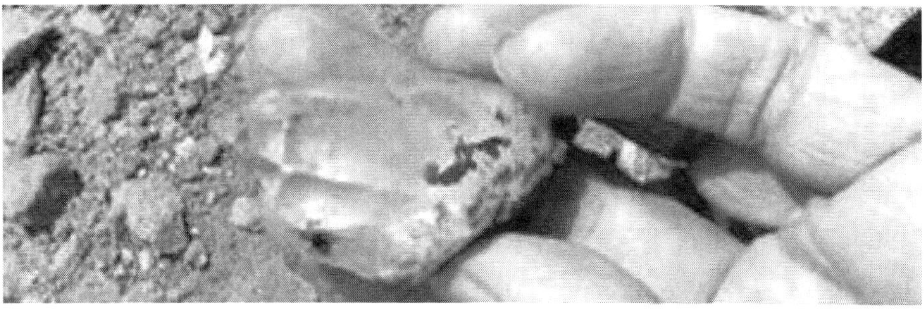

I find that if my head's not in the right space, I don't find very many crystals. I make it a point to remain in a space of thankfulness and gratitude. I usually like to walk off by myself even when digging with friends because I like to talk to the crystal as I'm digging.

When you're finished digging and ready to go home, the best way to pack your crystal for transport is with newspaper.

If you have used the zip top baggie suggestion, they can be placed side by side in the floor behind the seats. Clusters can be placed in a flat box with newspaper between them to prevent them from bumping each other.

If you are lucky and find a cluster with lots of clay on it in the fresh tailings, it is best to leave the clay on for protection until you can get it home. Resist the temptation to "unwrap" it from the clay, and it will remain safe.

As you dig, be respectful. You aren't going to be able to bring home every single crystal that you come across. Some crystals I know instinctively aren't for me. I have seen people mindlessly toss such crystals aside in the search for something *better*. Don't be one of these people!

When I find a crystal that isn't for me, I thank it, tell it how beautiful it is and set it prominently on a nearby rock so it will be easily found by the person it *is* meant for.

If the crystal is for me and it goes into my bucket, I don't just drop it in; I carefully place it in and thank it as I do so. I don't do this because I am afraid I will damage it by dropping it in, but more because to carelessly drop it in the bucket is disrespectful.

We talked about how I kiss the crystal before putting it in my bucket. I will continue to do that, even if it does make me look a little demented. I have a vision of myself through other people's eyes: this crazy girl walking around alone, mumbling away with dirt all around her mouth. Maybe this is why I like to walk away and dig by myself; it saves my friends the embarrassment of having to admit they know me!

After you wash off the dirt and clay, some crystal appears clean straight out of the mine (like it looks when you see it in shops). Most, however, is stained with rust which requires an acid bath to remove.

Plan to buy some acid at the rock shop to take home with which to clean your crystals. Generally it is one pound of acid to five gallons of water. Oxalic acid is a dry white powder and they sell it packaged by the pound.

While one pound is generally more than enough, you can ask the person running the rock shop what they recommend for the amount of crystal you found; they are very helpful. There is a process to using the acid, so be sure to ask for the instructions as well.

When you get your crystal home, you will need to wash it off well with water. The more clay and dirt you remove before putting it in the acid, the better. There are two reasons for this. Firstly if you don't, the crystal might require two trips through the acid and secondly, the less dirt you get in your acid, the better. It can be re-used until it gets saturated. When it turns a green color, it is time to throw it out. When finished, neutralize the acid with lime (the kind you buy for the garden) and use plenty of water.

If your crystal isn't heavily stained with iron, it should take only a few days in the acid bath to get it clean. Rinse the crystal well with water after you take it out. With all of these instructions, your common sense is your most valuable tool.

That concludes our chapter on digging crystal. I would say the single most important things to plan to bring with you to the mine are your gratefulness, respect and reverence, as well as your gratitude and respect for the crystal and your reverence to Mother Earth for enduring this birth process on our behalf. Most especially remember to bring your laughter and good vibes; this is a joyous endeavor!

Conclusion

The end of this book is what I call your beginning.

We've discussed many different topics. You should be amazed at the new knowledge you now possess!

- You've learned how crystal is formed and what the crystal mining process entails.

- You are now recognizing crystals as ancient beings.

- You discovered that crystal broadcasts on many different "channels" and you have determined which one is clearest for you.

- You know the importance of being a Lightworker and how essential you are to getting the crystal out to increase the vibration of humanity.

- You found out that crystal interacts with other beings.

- The nuts and bolts of crystal anatomy and configurations are now much easier for you to determine.

- You're familiar with the difference between cleansing and clearing, what a program is and how to do all three.

- You recognize that intent is paramount to successful co-creation with your crystal friend.

- You understand that your instinct is more important than anything you might read in a book.

- You've acquired knowledge about the many different ways crystal can assist in healing.

- You know how to use crystal grids.

- You learned how to make, and use, a variety of tools.

- You also know how, when, and where, to gather your own crystal.

- You should be proud of yourself because that's a lot of information!

Let's discuss a little bit more about finding crystals to work with.

If you live too far away to dig your own, there are plenty of great options available.

A perfectly acceptable way to look for your crystal is online. It's great if you have a person you trust where you know the crystal you are receiving has been respectfully gathered and continues to be respected throughout the adoption process.

Ask your friends where they obtained theirs. Read the bio and "about me" info on websites. Trust your gut. If a website gives you a good (or conversely a bad) feeling, trust that. Learning to hear the call from our crystal friends should be easier for you now that you know how to listen.

If you are being called by a crystal, you may feel a pull when you see a picture online. Alternately a crystal might call to you in a dream. A crystal may be gifted to you, or you may stumble across one in an estate sale or flea market.

Crystals can appear to us in the most unexpected places. Be open and ready to answer the call.

I have made more friends than I can count whom I never would have met if it weren't for the Crystal People. Be open to the new relationships to which the Crystal People lead you.

It is probable that at some point during your relationship with a crystal friend, it may inexplicably disappear. This happens often. It simply means that your time to learn from that particular crystal is complete and it is now time for the crystal to move on to the next person.

There are times when crystals come to us and times when they leave. Be aware that the call you hear from your crystal friend might be one of letting go.

At times, some of my favorite crystals request that I send them to a new home. It doesn't mean that I don't still love that crystal very much, I'm simply aware that it is needed by someone else more than it is needed by me. If you remember that we are always connected by our etheric cord, it makes physically parting less difficult; when it is time, you will know.

You've learned many ways to communicate with your crystal friend. You understand now that your relationship is one of co-creation.

The most important lessons you should take with you are to remember to have fun and interact with joy, maintain a strong heart connection, remain grateful and show them respect as ancient beings.

Now you know the Crystal People.

Appendix

I can be reached at genn@arkansascrystalworks.com

If you are looking for a specific crystal, or have a specific need, let me know.

As well, feel free to check out my website at www.arkansascrystalworks.com to see the crystals I have up for adoption.

As far as Crystal Digging in Arkansas goes, the information changes somewhat frequently and there are many mines from which to choose. My suggestion is that you check with the Mount Ida Chamber of Commerce. They have a current list of crystal mines and contact information for each mine.

Mount Ida Chamber of Commerce

124 Hwy 270 West, Mount Ida, Arkansas 71957

director@mtidachamber.com

870-867-2723

Works Cited

Holbrook, T. (2009, Sept 22). Face to Face with Ants. Retrieved from ASU School of Life Sciences Ask a Biologist: http://askabiologist.asu.edu/content/ant-factoids

Howard, M. (2011). Basic Mineral Identification. Retrieved Nov 14, 2012, from Rockhounding Arkansas http://rockhoundingar.com/basics.php

Howard, M. (2011). Geology and Mineralogy of Quartz Crystals. Retrieved Nov 14, 2012, from Rockhounding Arkansas http://rockhoundingar.com/mineralogy.php

Howard, M. (2011). Introducing the Geology of Arkansas. Retrieved Nov 14, 2012, from Rockhounding Arkansas http://rockhoundingar.com/geology.php

Howard, M. (2011). Quartz as Gems Colorless Quartz, also known as Rock Crystal. Retrieved Nov 14, 2012, from Rockhounding Arkansas http://rockhoundingar.com/qtzgems.php

Howard, M. (2011). Rocks and Minerals. Retrieved Nov 14, 2012, from Rockhounding Arkansas http://rockhoundingar.com/rocksandminerals.php

Howard, M. (2011). The Formation of the Ouachita Mountains. Retrieved Nov 14, 2012, from Rockhounding Arkansas http://rockhoundingar.com/ouamtns.php

Howard, M. (2011). The Geologic Time Scale, and a brief history of how Arkansas was made. Retrieved Nov 14, 2012, from Rockhounding Arkansas http://rockhoundingar.com/timescale.php

John C. Nichols, F. G. (1999, Jan 27). Minerals and Geology: Quartz on the Ouachita National Forest. Retrieved Nov 18, 2012, from USDA Forest Service Ouachita National Forest http://www.fs.usda.gov/

Mineralogical Society of America (1997-2006). COLLECTOR'S CORNER FREQUENTLY ASKED

QUESTIONS MINERALOGY - GENERAL. Retrieved Nov 15, 2012, from Mineralogical Society of America http://www.minsocam.org/msa/collectors_corner/faq/faqmingen.htm

Tyb`eronn, J. (2012, June 6). Issue # 46: Earth-Keeper Chronicles AA Metatron Channel : Revisiting Atlantis: The Crystalline Field of 10-10-10. Retrieved Nov 14, 2012, from Earth Keeper http://www.earth-keeper.com/EKnews_6-6-2010.htm

12815682R00198

Printed in Poland
by Amazon Fulfillment
Poland Sp. z o.o., Wrocław